STAND-UP DECODED

Copyright © 2014 by Lue Deck.

All rights reserved. No part of this book may be reproduced or transmitted in any form or by any means, electronic or mechanical, including photocopying, recording, or by any information storage and retrieval system, without permission in writing from the copyright owner.
This is a work of fiction. Names, characters, places and incidents either are the product of the author's imagination or are used fictitiously, and any resemblance to any actual persons, living or dead, events, or locales is entirely coincidental.

ISBN 13   978-1-64007-086-8
ISBN 10   1-64007-086-9

Rev. date: 10/16/2014

McNae, Marlin and MacKenzie Publishers, Ltd.
www.m3publishers.com

Contents

Dedications: 4

Grateful Acknowledgements 5

A Comic Manifesto 7

God Is Funny! 8

Huddled around some laughs! 10

Goodbye Mr. Carson 12

HEAVEN'S Comedy Club 15

I Shoulda Strangled Pauly Shore! 17

Herk and Jerk, the Saga of 20

What I Know That You don't! 24

The Last Honest Booking Agent! 26

The Greatest Star That Never Was! 30

Jokes or Attitude? 35

The Night nothing was funny! 37

Hell's Cruise Ship! 40

If I were King! 42

The Cop and the Comic! 43

He Made Me Do It! 45

How to Get Happy! 47

Grandpa's Promise 49

I'm Still Standing! 55

The Queen of Comedy! 58

CSPAN Called Me! 60

RENT MY BODY? 62

I told Me Not to Do it! 65

Things you should remember: 68

Curriculum Vitae 78

Captions: 79

Dedications:

These efforts are dedicated to the three most amazing women on the planet.

First, my Mother, who gave up her aspirations as a Barbershop quartet singer to raise three kids alone. She'll always be my biggest inspiration.

Second, Mitzi Shore, the whirlwind impresario who made L.A.'s Comedy Store world famous. Why she chose me is still her secret.

Third, My trusty little side-kick, Ms. Sara Tonin, who has made me so incredibly happy! She describes me as: white on top, red on the bottom and funny in the middle!

Thanks to you three for your love, guidance, and shiploads of your patience. I promise to stay out of trouble. Really, I've been good. *That's my story, and I'm still sticking to it.*

Last of all, to Lady Stand-up, The Goddess of laughter: Thanks for all the strange places you took me, and all the things I got to do. Thanks for teaching me. You led me to everything I ever wanted, and all you asked of me was to be funny. I gave you my youth, I gave you my soul, and you gave me the whole world. From the bottom of my heart: *I hope it was that good for you too!*

Grateful Acknowledgements

Jimmy Heck was my comedy duo partner for seven years. He is the bravest, funniest, and most dangerous two guys I've ever met.

The Comedy Store is the log cabin where my dreams were born and came true. If The Comedy Store needs help, just call. Many, many will always remember and answer.

David Letterman and Jay Leno: I studied you, emulated you, and wanted to be you! You are the best monologists on television since Johnny Carson. As I learned to be a stand-up comic, you taught me that the only character to play was myself. You trail-blazed the path for me and other comics to follow. We all owe you both many thanks!

Tom Sobel is my teacher, business pal, and friend. Tom is the best I ever saw. When I grow up, I want to be just like him, except for the bald part.

Bret Sohl was the soul of The Comedy Caravan in Louisville, KY for eleven years. He reminds me of me at that age, except that I was prettier and lots funnier, damn it! His seminar: "MC 101" was the best MC School since The Comedy Store in the 70's. Bret also sold more jokes to Jay's Tonight Show than anybody but Buddha. Thanks, Bret!

Department of Defense Overseas Tours: I was proud to serve. I am ready to be recalled. The Pentagon should award all Morale & Rec. guys more stripes and three "Atta boys!"

Geno Michellini of the "5 o'clock Funnies!" in L.A. helped me remember who I was, and what I'd accomplished. Thank you Gene. FM misses you! Boycott KLOS! Gene is more important than Geno! Now, I'm older, I want to be just like him, except for the bald part.

Net Radio Live inventor Jordan Dorf put me up for my first Peabody Award nomination. Thanks Jordan, for giving "Poor Lue's Almanac" just enough breathing room.

Susan Smith, CSPAN honcho, is the most humane person in reporting today. I was the first (in print) to call for Brian Lamb's Medal of Freedom. Susan agreed.

I sheepishly acknowledge that I would rather have had an old style and reputable publisher put my book out, but as a 21st century pragmatist, I knew if it was going to get done, I'd have to do it my damn self.

The Cheers.org has copyrighted and originally (and generously) published all my essays herein. The pride of Tallinn, Estonia: Siim Einfeldt is the only editor I've ever had, and he can laugh at my jokes in five languages! As a columnist, Siim raised me from a pup, so naturally, my bark is worse than my bite. Pallun, my friend, Pallun!

A Comic Manifesto

Show me the funny! I'm addicted to making people laugh. For my whole career, I've never been able to stop feeding my need to make people laugh. For me, it's all about the funny!

So, you think you're funny. That's good. Thanks for checking this out. If you don't think you're funny, then stop reading this! Stop! These insights are for me and my funny kind. Not You. Ours is a war against the powers that don't laugh. Go away! (You funny folks, hang on a moment.) If you don't think you are funny, go try something else. Go join a hypocritical political party and invade somewhere. Stop reading! Go away! This is only for people who think they are funny.

Where was I? Oh yeah, funny. Can I teach you how to be funny? I don't think so. But I do know that funny can be coached. If you know you're funny, then logically, you can learn to be funnier. Doing stand-up comedy is all about the choices you make. No matter where you are in your stand-up career, you will need to make better choices, always.

Stand-up stage craft is both an art, and a science. You should study both, and also its history. My efforts here are mainly to help you teach yourself how to be a better stand-up comic. If this sounds like a linguistics course, it kinda is. Each essay is intended to expose and explain certain facets of a stand-up's repertoire. Working stand-up comics, like members of The Marine Corps, need to adapt, improvise, and overcome obstacles every day. Now, so do you!

Perhaps you can save yourself some time with some of the lessons I've learned along my way. To be fair, I have to warn you: Getting funnier has consequences, and is very addicting.

I believe if you give a man a laugh, then he laughs today. If you give a man the right tools to make others laugh, he (and they) laugh every day!

God Is Funny!

When you're talking about God, it can be a difficult concept to grasp. Just think about it. Whether it's your God…or my God…or anyone else's God, whichever or whatever you want to picture, it's gotta be **tough to be GOD!** All right, for a moment, picture yourself as God. (For Martha Stewart, Simon Cowl, and Kanye West, this suggestion may be redundant.) Again, picture yourself **AS God:**

Wow, just listen to all those souls constantly calling for help. And all those holidays keep coming and coming…your voice mail is always chock full….And always, always having to do the right thing…Is Armageddon this millennium, or the next one…The Devil's relentless shenanigans…repeated knocks at your bedroom door, just as you were finally falling asleep, at last…flood here, drought there…heal this one, save that one, do nothing for that one. Gee, that's a **lot of pressure** building upon you!

So, what does God do to have fun and relax? Well, since Albert Einstein made his famous remark about playing dice, God can't even slip into Las Vegas and shoot craps anymore. (You see, not everything that happens in Vegas stays in Vegas.)

It's my belief God visits Earth to work on His own stand-up comedy act. Of course, God headlines for St. Peter's Comedy Club at The Pearly Gates. It's His home stage, but it's real tough to get a good read on material there. So, to test His newest stuff, God descends to Earth, and works as the feature (middle) act, or, **Himself** forbid, or as the MC/Opening act.

God knows our modern format for a three act stand-up show is: MC/ Opener doing fifteen minutes, the feature act performs for thirty minutes, and the headliner stays on forty-five to fifty minutes. He knows this, because God and Mitzi Shore first invented said format in 1974 for The Comedy Store in LaJolla, CA. They knew that stand-up crowds get tired after 90-95 minutes, and don't laugh as much. God never goes over on his time; besides, if God wanted to, He could do two hours, and make it seem like just thirty minutes to the audience and booker. After all, He is the omniscient one.

God gets stage time *almost* anywhere he wants. (But, in Los Angeles, The Laugh Factory, and Improv operate on the old "It's **who** you **know**" system, and these days, they don't seem know Him anymore.)

God instead, prefers the independent clubs with sole proprietors. The stinkin' one-nighter chains like The Comedy Zones and Laff Stops; He wouldn't be caught dead in those sink holes. For stand-up workouts, God **avoids** both coasts, concentrating on The Mid-West and The South. (Mostly because He knows that's where the really big laughs are.) Never in Miami for some reason. Ask him why.

God usually appears amongst us as folks that are skilled enough to make us laugh, but other than that, not quite striking enough to be distinctly memorable. You laughed last night, but right now, you can't picture His face. That's the beauty of His plans! But, His guys do still sell a lot of T-shirts. Go figure.

It's a well-known fact that God always does a whole lot of observational stuff. He rarely resorts to the old "Where're you from" bit…comic Jimmy Brogan is King of "playing the crowd." Brogan's schtick was so well known; his CA license plate read "**NO ACT!**" Anyhoo, God knows exactly where you're from.

You would think more people would recall God's act, because He usually does so well. I think God frequently does rap parodies, because He knows if He does rap parodies, nobody, anywhere, will ever remember any comic doing rap! Again, remarkably, that's the depth and beauty of His plan for us all.

Once, some years back, they booked God as the rookie feature act in Birmingham, Alabama with the leading prop hack of the time, Carrot Top! During an unexpected blizzard, the entire club (with all of Carrot head's props) burned to the ground!

Just who says: GOD IS NOT FUNNY??

So, one evening, after you leave your local comedy club, if you just happen to have this really great feeling, and are extra happy for no reason, and you can't figure out why…Maybe, just maybe, you had been blessed, and you got to see God try out His newest jokes! **All** God's chilluns' need to keep laughing!

Lesson one: If God Almighty can get off his scrawny butt to write, and go try out his newest jokes, then so can you! New jokes make the stand-up world go around. You'll only get out of it, what you put into it. Get a box full of courage and be very loud for your first ten shows. Put a lot of effort in, so you can get a lot out. Tactics, techniques, and procedures can help a lot. It's on you to make this whole thing work. And remember: Never, ever do rap!

Huddled around some laughs!

(How we got to where we are)

Actually we, the modern day equivalent of caveman, cavewomen, and cave kiddies, are all just looking to lean towards a friendly fire. Except that my peeps...my kinda folks...the people that I want to talk to...are all huddled around some laughs! In a tainted world, what could be a greater equalizer than mocking the very thing that threatens us? Mankind is hard-wired to relieve its stress by laughing in the face of danger! Maybe laughing a lot is the fountain of youth! Maybe.

I envision it all started long ago in a half darkened cave, on a wild and breezy night. Heralding the future of man, Errrg the caveman had had a rough, rough day-day! Maybe Errrg lived in the hinterlands of Australia, perhaps near Sidney, or in some crazy peat bog in Estonia, near Tallinn. I don't know, and I don't care. What I see in my mind's eye is...mostly; my man Errrg had a horrible day. After a meager dinner, and also fed up to here with Mrs. Errrg, Errrg Junior, and Gramma Gas, he wandered over to the communal fire to commiserate a little. You know, the Cro-Magnon version of water cooler talk: "Wow, it's a damn tar-pit out there! Hey, how about those T-Rexes? " One might have heard such talk.

So, Errrg sidles up to the comforting flames, palms out, in a tribal gesture still seen today in New York City. His next cave neighbor, Drooog, cuts a huge one, and hoots loudly. Catcalls come from all angles. Errrg comments dryly: "Windy tonight, huh?" Drooog shoots Errrg a look worthy of a modern day Frenchman receiving a very small tip. Curious, Drooog asks of all those fireside: "Has the mighty Errrg had a bad day?" Errrg waits for the crowd to quiet, then he says: "Don't laugh, one day I'll have a series of TV ads, and my own network sit-com!"

Drooog looks puzzled, so Errrg adds: "Drooog, you're the only one in the tribe that can drool, sneeze, and break wind, all at the same time...but you're totally useless on the hunt! I'm surprised the women let you come down and stand out here with us men! Do I come down to the Poop Pits, and screw up your job?" Shouts, insults, and much munched-on bones rain down on poor Drooog as he slinks away from Errrg and all at the fire. And so, stand-up comedy, as we know it, had begun.

Later, in the Middle Ages, comedic banter contributed to The Holy Land being exchanged through conquest several times. As apparently discovered then, and forevermore recorded in the secret journals and rituals of funnymen since: *"Some people can't take a joke!"* This includes evangelists, popes, dictators, Customs officials, online magazine editors, motorcycle cops, taxi drivers, airport gate agents, some waitresses, research doctors, some lesbians, and The NSA.

Let history now confirm: Moses, Jesus, Mohammed, Confucius, and Buddha were all quite funny.

Later, during the Renaissance, provoking laughter was a highly sought after skill, second only to Inquisition assistants. The Medici's and the Sir Williams of Morris were some of the most revered and remembered patrons. Off-duty jesters were given menial tasks to keep them out of trouble during daytime hours. Cleaning castle walls led to our modern phrase "These guys are just "sponging" off the Duke!

There was nothing funny about the 1700's, and mostly, people everywhere suffered greatly.

In the 18 and early 1900's, making folks laugh was considered a sign of up-to-no-goodness. Mark Twain, Will Rogers, Charlie Chaplin, Harold Lloyd changed that. Then Fatty Arbuckle came along and changed our reputation back to up-to-no-good...again. Thanks a lot.

Then Earth was blessed, and when burlesque, vaudeville, radio, and TV realized they could sell laughs like they were hot bagels, and it was off to the races! After the comedy rush of the 80's and 90's, standup comics gained exposure and stature…and a decent paycheck. Soon, anybody who disrupted a high school class, or held sway at a beer bust thought they could be a stand-up too. The art form and business wobbled, but it has survived. I think the fact that the fake TV show *Last Comic Standing!* looked like death warmed over, is a good sign. There may be some magic left yet.

American General MacArthur said: "There is no substitute for victory!" Today, there is no substitute for getting good laughs than by visiting your local comedy club. An evening at a decent live comedy show is a victory that can do amazing things for you. The actual act of laughing for any extended period of time heals and cleanses the human system like no other act but love-making. So, if you can't make love tonight, or any particular night…how about some laughs? Bring her! Or him. Come join us! It's not hard to find a good show almost anywhere these days. If you want to test the holistic and beneficial results, drive past your local comedy club as the audience leaves a show. These exiting folks are happy, and ready to deal with whatever tomorrow brings. Judge for yourself. Do you want a piece of this? Come on in, and have a giggle or two. You'll see the rest of us, we're having fun down at The Comedy Cave…we're huddled around some laughs!

Lesson two: You need to develop a Punch line bell in your head. As a newbie stand-up comic, my jokes became as important to me as food, money, or sex. When I made my pals laugh, I began to notice why they laughed, how I provoked their laugh, and when, in our give and take, did I see the chance to go for the laugh. (Was it an adlib, or a joke I wrote?) On my weekly review day, I would bear that in mind and think aloud in joke formula until I made myself laugh, then I'd visualize and try to actually hear a bell ring. This high-lighted the moment and reminded me to write the thought (or possible joke) down immediately. You have to actually write a joke down, not just think about it. When my punch line bell rings, it signals my joke factory that the raw materials are here. Write all those ideas down.

Goodbye Mr. Carson.

In World War Two, a Dear John letter meant someone was getting kissed off. This is not that kind of letter, but it is a Dear John letter, and someone is getting kissed off. Other than that, it's not that kind of letter. Today, when I woke up, I heard Johnny Carson had died. The Golden Age of Comedy has definitely ended! Mr. Carson starred on and produced The Tonight Show. That meant Johnny was his own boss. He didn't have to worry about the small stuff. But, he did. As an entire generation of comic actor types got older, Carson made them relevant again in the seventies and eighties. Don Rickles, Buddy Hackett, Charles Grodin, and many more got career extensions from breaking up Johnny at his desk. Rodney Dangerfield got another chance on The Tonight Show, which he played to the hilt.

When The Tonight Show moved to the west coast, it was like a golden spotlight had suddenly lit up the staircase used by stand-up comedians. Standing at the top of that staircase was Johnny Carson. And he was helping young comics, defining, where none had existed before, a methodology for them to follow his footsteps. It was the most gracious thing ever done on TV, and in stand-up comedy history. Carson defined and knighted his own stylish Band of Brothers. Dave Letterman, Jay Leno, Steve Martin, Billy Crystal, Jerry Seinfeld, Arsenio Hall, David Brenner, David Steinberg, and many more of his chosen, sat at King Carson's Round Table. It was heady stuff!

As the second or third comedy wave broke on the west coast beaches, bringing various flotsams into the L.A. stand-up scene, I washed ashore. On my first day, I landed a job at The World Famous Comedy Store. Then I took three buses to get to Burbank for a taping of the Tonight show. I made the acquaintance of a marvelous young lady, also waiting in line. It happened to be the night Johnny did the infamous Rhinestone Cowboy gag, riding a three-foot tall burro. Wow, hey Johnny, I'm in show biz, too! We waited in her car on the street, and stalked Mr. Carson, the whole way to his Bellaire home. No charges were filed against us.

A year later, I was a regular at the Comedy Store. Actually, I was an MC and doorman. But, after being chosen by the owner to host shows, I was there virtually every night. We were having music in the largest of the three showrooms that weekend. Buddy Rich and his Orchestra had pulled a full house in our Main Room. I bumped into Mr. Carson in the men's room. He didn't remember me. Trying not to get Mr. Carson wet, I told him I had noticed that Jeff Altman, a favorite, was now onstage in the smaller Original Room, and was just about to do his great Johnny Carson impression. Making a spraying exit, Johnny led his entourage into the smaller room, just in time to see Jeff's bit. Altman took a bow as he finished the bit, but didn't notice Johnny step to the stage. As the crowd recognized Carson and began applauding, Jeff thought the reaction was for him. Turning, he sees Johnny and realizes his mistake. They both share the laugh. Then, Jeff introduces Johnny onstage, hands him the mike, and exits right to me at the back of the room. I told Jeff, he had achieved the near impossible. Johnny Carson would now be, in perpetuity, a Comedy Store regular.

Five years later, several comics had hired me to coach them through their first Tonight Show appearances. Skip Stephenson, Reverend George Wallace and Argus Hamilton had all asked me to accompany them backstage. All three did extremely well. Although Mr. Carson said Hi, he didn't seem to place me. Just four days later, I was sweeping the sidewalk in front, prior to opening The Comedy Store. A fancy green Mercedes pulled up in front of me and, Lo and Behold, Johnny Carson got out! And he wanted to talk to ME. Evidently, he did remember me, because he asked to use our bathroom. When he came out, he made a point of inviting me to a taping of his show, anytime, and then drove right off.

Three years later, I had been performing in a revue show in Reno. I had to exit a 40-yard stage in the dark, and kept falling into the orchestra pit. I started wearing red shoes, so I could see my feet. I stopped falling in the orchestra pit. No biggie. When I got back to The Comedy Store two weeks later, I was still wearing them. I was standing around, chatting up the guys, when an act didn't show. So, I got to fill in for the ten-minute spot. I probably had the best show I had ever done in the Original Room. There's nothing like some shows on the road to sharpen your act. When I exited the stage, I flew down the back steps, right into Mr. Carson. I was sputtering apologies, when Johnny Carson himself, brushed himself off, stuck out his hand, and said: "Nice set, Lue! I didn't know you even did stand-up! Good stuff! And, those red shoes are wild! Great idea, Lue! Distinctive footwear!" It made the eighties for me. Johnny Carson liked my act. And my Red Shoes! There is a God!

Mr. Carson influenced more comics than you will ever know. From Richard Pryor to Robin Williams. And many, many others in between. He taught us to get our best shots in, while using less than six minutes. He taught us that the best parts of us didn't express profane language on TV. But, mostly he taught us that class pays off. He taught comics to envision themselves big, REAL BIG. And calling their own shots. The trouble is, no comic has ever envisioned himself or herself as big as Johnny Carson. Not even Johnny! Who could? Really, when I heard that Johnny Carson died, I knew The Golden Age of Comedy had definitely ended. Now, it's up to his heirs to start a new era. Maybe it has started already. We'll see. But, I'll miss your sincerity and most of all, your warmth! Thanks! We won't ever forget you. Goodbye, Mister Carson.

Lesson three: Get a spiral bound notebook or steno pad. Write down all the funny thoughts or ideas you have this week. Then, one day a week, review what you've written. Develop your best ideas into real jokes. Do all these things until you've filled three notebooks. Congratulations! Now you've built your very own joke factory. This is where your jokes come from.

You can write a joke, make a joke, perform a joke, and be a joke. Learn the difference and you'll have three more weapons in your stand-up arsenal. Your first jokes should be about you. Your next jokes should be about how you handle life. Your next jokes should be about situations you share with your audiences. Your next jokes should be about the society in which you live. Your next jokes should be about how you overcome your obstacles. Your next jokes should be about you. Get it?

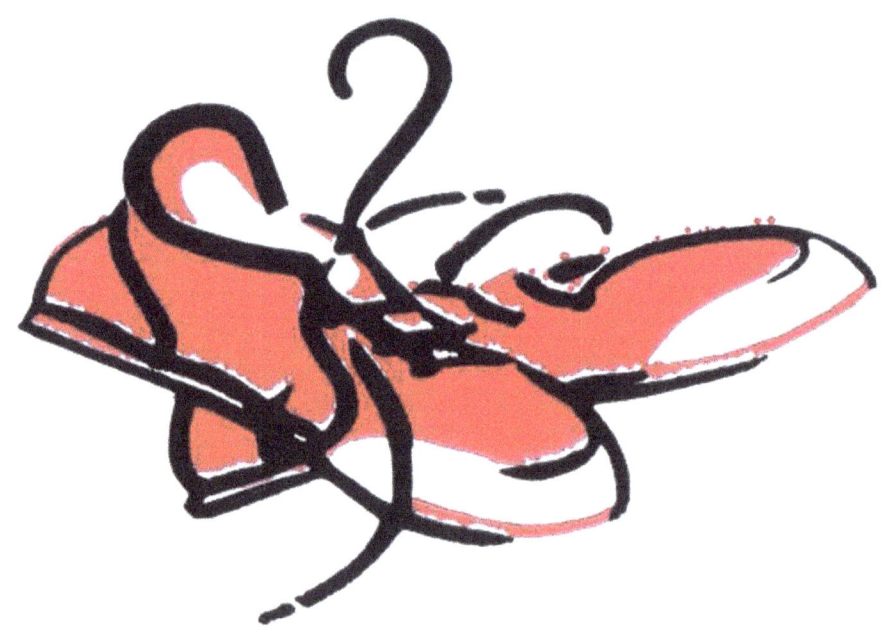

HEAVEN'S Comedy Club

I know there such a thing as a comedy heaven! Some say there's a place between heaven and hell. In my own quirky way, I believe that this place will turn out to be St. Peter's Comedy Club at the Pearly Gates!

I envision a spot for all the people who were very sad, or too busy, or just overwhelmed by life's ceaseless churning. After St. Peter and his doorman crew clear you through the metal detectors, you too can come on in to see the stand-up comedy show that never fails.

Somewhere during the selection process for Heaven or Hell, St. Peter checks everyone's laugh meter. If any individual registers too low on his guffaw scale, St. Peter ordains a visit to his comedy club. You'd be surprised how many lost souls really need some laughs. Our main room is usually packed for almost every performer. "Hi there… Come on in!"

Walking in, notice this is a big room. (We don't say Vegas-style up here.) The first hundred seats up front are kept in reserve for folks who were cowered or so sad while on Earth. These sections are almost always full. We'll go over to the bar (yes, we have one) to have a cool one and scope our peeps out. One can see a lot here at St. Peter's club on any given evening, and the joint is certainly jumping tonight. "Hey, you've got good timing!"

Our dearest bartender is Buddha! He tells us the jokes he's heard here for years have always enlightened him. I say "Hi!" and order us two lotus daiquiris. "Hey, look over there, see that recessed booth with the back light? Looks like Andy Kaufman is arguing with Tony Clifton over something insane and they got Gilda Radnor and Freddy Prinze in stitches!" For *my* karma, I leave Buddha a twenty.

At the scheduling desk, Redd Fox is reserving a spot for Richard Pryor. Bob Hope, Shelley Berman and Imogene Coca are seconding the motion. Master of Ceremonies Flip Wilson consults with Killer, then agrees. Buddy Hackett pulls Phil Silvers pants down, and they all laugh real hard! Old school at its best!

On the other side of the bar, Joey Bishop and Milton Berle are planning to play a practical joke on Red Skelton. What they don't notice is, Red, at this very moment is lighting the left foot of both on fire, with a double classic hotfoot!

The Marx Brothers (minus Harpo, who is, appropriately enough, in the back playing his harp) are dealing Texas Hold 'Em to the Three Stooges. It's the only time I've ever seen poker with seltzer bottles and cream pies. Watch out! Hot stuff, comin' through!

"See that table towards the back? It's Lucille Ball, Rose Marie, Shirley Hemphill, and Moms Mabley. They're all listening to Jack Benny explaining why Bill Hicks was so funny, and they're all hooting quite loudly. See the booth behind them? It's Paul Lynn, who's trying to convince WC Fields that Will Rogers was really quite gay."

"What did you say? I couldn't hear you. No, we won't get to see Sam Kennison. He's been playing at our other club. You know, the one just over the River Styx, in Hades. It's just as well, because lots of his loyal followers go there too. I've been told that other club features singing waitresses. Now, that's Hell!"

Check out our stage. We've got the best light and sound system in the business. We got it from the Ice House in Pasadena, CA! They've always been good to comics. Wait, Rodney Dangerfield is just finishing his set. It's no surprise that Rodney always gets his respect here. I give him the OK sign. Thanks Mr. Roy.

The only hecklers we allow are our fellow comics joshing their pals. We have a two "good deed" minimum here, but almost everybody pre-pays on earth. Our show lineup isn't ever announced, but, it is electric in here. "Something special can happen tonight! Keep your eyes peeled and your ears tuned in, all right?"

Some friends in the corner, wave and tell us that Lenny Bruce and Steve Allen each did sets earlier, and wrecked the place. Boy, I wish we could've seen that! Looking around, I see a lot of familiar faces in attendance. John Belushi and John Candy are having an eating contest in the VIP booth. That could get ugly!

A big roar from the stage gets my attention. As I look over my shoulder, I see Morey Amsterdam has finished with his big cello, and has just introduced Johnny Carson. Johnny has been working out almost every night since his recent arrival. With his naïve "I'm from Nebraska" attitude, he's got the crowd eating out of his hand. *"So, I'm kissing my girl, and she asks me if I've got any protection.* I tell her: *We're in the middle of a cornfield; we'll see 'em comin'!* ...*If it makes you feel better, I got a shotgun in the truck!"* Huge laughs ensued. I know so many of his fans will always miss the King of late-night.

Yeah that's the way it is around here at St. Peter's Comedy Club at the Pearly Gates. We have a lot of laughs. It's not a bad gig to work…for all eternity. If you ever find yourself in our neighborhood, drop by and have some laughs with us!

Lesson four: Practice your mouth work. I know that I have to pronounce a new joke at least five times until my mouth is used to saying it the way I want to say it. For every three jokes I string together, I have to say those three in a row, at least five times, until my mouth is used to saying it the way I want it to sound. Work your mirror. (At least one out of the five times you practice new jokes, look at yourself in the mirror as you practice them. Maybe you might want to add a supporting expression or two.

I Shoulda Strangled Pauly Shore!

(It might have saved The Comedy Store!)

(Normally, I do not advocate violence of any kind…but this little…weasel, is a very special case.)

It all started when Elvis Presley's opening act, East Coast comic Sammy Shore, and his bride Mitzi opened our planet's first ALL comedy nightclub in Los Angeles, California. The Comedy Store on Sunset Blvd. was born in April, 1972. Sammy and Mitzi also had three kids, maybe you've heard of one of them. (Mitzi sold cigarettes and gum to raise extra cash.)

In May, 1972, (just one month later) Johnny Carson moved his *Tonight Show* into the now famous Burbank studios. An ironic twist of fate, that, as now the gathering wave of new stand-ups were just about to crash massively and loudly on Hollywood's strange Shores. (Pardon the pun, I couldn't help it!) The Lettermans, Lenos, Brenners, Gallaghers, Gabe Kaplans, and Robert Klein's all washed into the showcase scene, and with no hoopla, I followed them onto their beachhead. (At that point, nobody had told me yet that I wasn't funny. Not even Mitzi.)

Soon, the luring call of gigs on the road summoned Sammy, and after the divorce, Mitzi got the kids, the house on the 2nd tier of the Hollywood hills, and finally, sole control of the soon-to-be World Famous Comedy Store on Sunset Boulevard. I started working for her around then. It was like getting a full boat scholarship to Comedy College. I was now one of "Mitzi's boys!"

After expanding the Store in 1976, Mitzi opened the world's first whole-week comedy club, featuring an opening act who also acted as MC, a middle act (soon to be headliner) then capping it with the best "nobody" comics in the biz. (They weren't nobodies long!) La Jolla was a ritzy beach suburb of San Diego, and The Comedy Store South would soon debut the next incredible set of funny people, preparing for Las Vegas and TV stardom. The Robin Williamses, the Howie Mandels, the Jimmy Walkers (Dy-no-mite) and the Steve Landesburgs (Detective Dietriech on Barney Miller), all developed under The Store's and Mitzi's protective shield. They were the talented ones. And there were more.

Then, Mitzi opened her Westwood club, so her other stand-up acts could work out the kinks and add a little class, as far away as possible from the TV scouts. I started there, unheralded, unskilled, and unfed, as her assistant, doorman, and go get me this or that-er. On my first mission as her driver, I had to go pick up her kids from elementary school. That's when Pauly Shore first entered my life. I could've strangled him then. But, what did I know then? Nothing!

I used to tell two jokes about the" heir apparent" at The Comedy Store:

When I got back to L.A. after ten years on stand-up tour: *"Nobody knows me in Hollywood anymore! "I'm going to strangle Pauly Shore! And then, when I get out of prison… everybody will like me, and give me lots of gigs!"*

"Remember those Heaven's Gate cultists in San Diego, who committed mass suicide right before the comet showed up? The cultists dressed in Nike running outfits with new sneakers, castrated themselves, and committed suicide! When the Police showed up, they knew something was very, very wrong.…because there was a Pauly Shore movie playing in the DVD!"

As the years passed working in my chosen profession, I performed for pay in almost every state, and 34 other countries. Pauly Shore starred in *"Son-in-Law"*, *"In the Army now"*, *"Bio-Dome"* and the unbelievably successful *"Encino Man."* I went on to do stand-up shows in 1000 cities in 10 years, Pauly did his own show on TBS! I was nominated for a Peabody Award for my Internet radio show. Pauley has now inherited The Comedy Store brand. Where did I go wrong? I could have done things differently. I could've! I shoulda strangled Pauly long ago. But, it's too late now.

Now, since the Queen of Standup Comedy, Mitzi Shore, has grown very ill, the day-to-day operations might depend on a character named The Weasel! What has the world of stand-up come to? Well, that's life. My whole point is that even though Pauly has portrayed some less than likable parts on TV, and in the movies, his biggest challenge ever will be to play the leader of the funniest place on Earth.

Since Mitzi got sick, The Comedy Store has begun to fade a bit. Many comics, who called the club home then, now look back and wish her, and her kids: Pauly, Peter, and Sandy well! Not that we're coming back. Most aren't. I feel about The Comedy Store, the same way a combat hardened Marine feels about enduring boot camp at Paris Island: "Whew!...Thanks for the training!...Semper Funny!"

Like all of Mitzi's various alumni and graduates, I still care. Call us, if you need help! And good luck Pauly! I hope nobody strangles you.

Lesson five: This linguistic, vocational skill called stand-up comedy, sometimes masquerades as an art form, sometimes as an unbelievable farce. Although they represent opposite ends of the stand-up spectrum, Pauly Shore and Andrew Dice Clay are unique, and usually hazardous to emulate.

Remember: From the time the MC announces your name as the next act onstage, you have five or six seconds to take center stage and have the crowd recognize you are ready to make them happy.

Herk and Jerk, the Saga of

(A story of a young, ill-fated comedy team. The names of these stand-up comics involved here have been dramatically altered to protect those who were innocent…but in truth, I'm Jerk!)

Once upon a time, in a land far away called Texas, there began a comedy team named Herk and Jerk. One was small and angry with lots of red hair, while the other was tall, loud, and quite crazy. These two were zany, and energetic, and almost as if by accident…and often, Herk and Jerk were ***laugh out loud*** funny!

But mostly, they'd argue under their breath, then, one would up and smack the other one, and then a quick chase would ensue. A wry comment or two would be hurled, they'd laugh, and then settle down back to the chore at hand. Such was life in Herk & Jerk Land.

One of them just wanted to be funny; the other just wanted to be rich. Peering, with 20-20 hindsight, way back to then, it doesn't matter which wanted which. Poor little guys, they had no idea that most comedy teams break up, because the only way two comics can live on one paycheck is with a whole lot of useless fighting. Again, such was life in their obscure niche of this crazy old world.

One day, because, you know…life just wasn't tough enough in Texas, Herk and Jerk decided to move to Hollywood and try their hand at the professional show biz racquet. With Lens-Crafter's-like clarity, we can all look back and realize, even then, around eleven hundred and eighty hopeful souls barge into Los Angeles **every** bleeping day. But these two wackos were sure they would do OK. I wish I could warn them even now. But life don't work that way.

With a sleight of hand and a twist of fate, Jerk actually got a job as MC, and Mitzi's assistant on the bed of nails that was The World Famous Comedy Store. Herk got a job there too, answering phones, until he scheduled one too many 9 a.m. meetings for the late-rising owner. In the mid 70's, the art, as well as the hardcore business of selling one's stand-up act, was booming large at all of the industry showcase clubs, but the Sunset Comedy Store was the prime hot spot to hit the big time on TV. Many there hit it big.

These were formative times for Herk and Jerk. Having more than fifteen clubs welcome them to open their shows, our fellas began to do private gigs, including a pilot's fly-in at the famous castle in Lancaster, CA. H & J were so excited to get paid two hundred whole dollars, they worked off some tensions with their pilot, while she tried to do her pre-flight checklist. Herk found the T-bar, used to pivot the front landing wheel, and began to measure his cranial width, while Jerk tried to sneak the team bong aboard. Flustered on the ground, the lady pilot was worse in the air. At landing, she stalled at about twenty feet, and the Cessna slapped the ground, rolling only ten yards. Herk freaked out and refused to perform. "Hey, this was how Lynard Skynard died!" Jerk went on alone and did OK. The next day, the same woman insisted she fly Herk and Jerk home herself. Herk freaked even louder this time. So, do you two little boys still want to be in show business?

About this time, our favorite nuts, H & J wrote one of their feature routines: "How to roll the **perfect joint!**" An innovative, Monty Python inspired gag, with Herk announcing the methodology, and Jerk donning a Volkswagen-size baggie, and becoming the weed itself. H & J did an enlarged version of this bit, when they opened for the visionary punk band: The Dickies at The Whisky a Go-go.

Punk fans of the time rejected everything and advocated violence. Hundreds of pissed off punks began to verbally abuse our two heroes, and crowded onto that famous stage. Herk & Jerk lived to see another funny day only because, as Herk reached the climax of the whole gag, he substituted for the striking match with a regulation road flare. If the oncoming punks hadn't been stunned with the ferocity and heat of the moment, as well as the spouting fire from the road flare, Herk would not have been able to cover Jerk's hopping exit and narrow escape. The lesson here was to be prepared for your shows. If you do a show for The NRA, don't go onstage until you get a gun too.

As mental and financial problems started to plague our nutty boys, several breaks came their way. Richard Pryor was all over The Comedy Store on Sunset and so were Herk and Jerk. At the Ye Little Club in Beverly Hills, Joan Rivers' spot to work out her new jokes, Herk and Jerk opened the show when Diane Keaton rehearsed the two songs she would later sing in the movie *Annie Hall!*

When The Rolling Stones released the controversial album: *Black and Blue,* Herk and Jerk responded in a similar tone with their infamous song parody: *Violence is a Girl's Best Friend!* The opening lyrics are listed here for historical posterity. (Sung to the tune of *Diamonds are a Girl's Best Friend!*)

SOME HANDCUFFS WITH LACE, MIGHT BE QUITE CONTINENTAL

BUT, VIOLENCE IS A GIRL'S BEST FRIEND. A SLAP IN THE FACE…

FROM AN ORIENTAL IS OH, SO NICE…PLEASE DO IT TWICE!

MEN GROW OLD, WHEN BOTTOMS GROW COLD, CUZ WE ALL LIKE

TO SPANK ON THAT END. BUT, SQUARE CUT, OR PEAR SHAPE

THESE SHOCKS DON'T LOSE THEIR TASTE…CUZ,

VIOLENCE IS A GIRL'S BEST FRIEND!

Are you getting my drift here? These two escapees from *The Twilight Zone* thought outrageousness can be funny. Back then, it was.

One dark day, most of the newly famous comedians decided to blackmail the showcase industry into paying gigs. Most L.A. acts went on strike against the clubs who couldn't, or wouldn't pay.

When push came to shove, as it almost always did between these two knuckleheads, Herk and Jerk experienced this quasi-pseudo labor dispute, the same way they did everything else. One went one way, and the other, the other. One chose schizophrenia and supported the strike, the other chose his delusions, and supported The Comedy Store. This, despite a chance to play with The Comedy Store basketball team in The Los Angeles Forum, sadly heralded the last of the zany performing days of that scrappy twosome, Herk and Jerk. Again, which did which, is lost to history, and really unimportant.

What is important, though each went his own way, is what they shared: the courage, the desire, and the huevos to leave the known, and chase their dreams in the unknown. What they shared is alive and well, more than 40 years later. They were and still are a unique Band of Brothers. OK, I'll admit, maybe a quite looney little Band of Brothers.

I pity the fools abed, who must hold their manhood cheap, that they did not stand with Herk and Jerk in that St. Crispin's' Day caldron. Thanks, Herk! The spirit of Herk and Jerk is STILL out there. Long live those brave comedy soldiers. Long life to all those who risk what they have, every day, to move towards their deepest dreams…at any cost.

Lesson six: Don't perform for family and friends until you're ready. Listen to this! Have a plan for your set. Make a joke list. I use a key word system. Each joke is represented by one or two key words on your list. In a shorter set, your key words should all fit on one a 3x5 card for easy reference. You can always stare at your set list a couple of hundred times before you go onstage.

What I Know That You don't!

Scolding amateur comedians is hazardous. As I traveled in my own stand-up career, often I've been asked to help and coach some inexperienced comedy performers. If these wayward souls could be helped, mostly I tried to help. If I couldn't help, then I gave encouragement. A lot of comics certainly helped me. Lord, I wish I could have helped all of them. There seem to be more inept stand-ups than good ones.

Having seen, at three meter range, the evolution of Andrew "Dice" Clay, Sam Kinison, and Yakov Smirnov, I underscore here, there are roughly two kinds of comics. There are joke-telling comics, and there are the character or "attitude" comics. My advice here is primarily for the joke tellers. If you're attempting to do an "attitude" act, I can't offer any advice: except acting lessons or seeing a psychologist. It would have helped Sam Kinison; it might still help "Dice" Clay. This stuff won't help ventriloquists! In my opinion, nothing can help ventriloquists. Nothing.

If you are reading this, and you're not a comic, quit peeking! I apologize for my tone. I am harsh, but newbie comics need to learn fast, for all our sakes. Besides, I just don't want to argue with beginners who don't know what I know. I've morphed many conversations with rookie stand-ups into my very personal list of do's and don'ts that work for almost all comics, so listen up, you arrogant little snots. Pay heed:

Performing standup comedy is another bizarre form of public speaking. Most of the rules of public speaking apply to stand-up, except in stand-up you can choose to add in some charm, mischief, or even an idiosyncrasy! See George Lopez, Rosie O'Donnell, or Dane Cook.

The absolute essence of doing stand-up is your likeability. If the audience does like you, they'll laugh at your weakest stuff. If they don't like you, they'll only laugh when you provoke or challenge them, if at all. Methods to accomplish this are similar to the behavior you exhibit while hosting a dinner party for your grandmother, or meeting your date's dad, or even applying for a highly paid job. Think brown-noser to the second power.

If you understand acting nice is *vital*, then add to that: **Look NICE!** If you achieve anything in your career, you'll be performing for paying customers. It's their night out, so I believe you owe them an effort to look as nice as the money they paid to see you. That's why it's called Show Biz. The crowd wants the show to look nice, and everybody putting on the show wants to get their pay, because after all, done correctly, this whole crazy idea is actually a business.

Learn to enter and leave the stage distinctively! Smile, wave, and find a way to build a focus (a focus is the necessary attention from the crowd to make your opening joke work) in five to eight seconds! (I start all of my shows by saying: "*HI, my name is Lue, if you would, everybody say "HI LUE!*") It's only human nature for people to do this and when they all respond in unison; they've effectively appointed me "Captain of NOW!" That's how I build focus, in just five to eight seconds. Invent a method for you to do something like that. It helps make your opening jokes work.

An act has three parts: the opening, the middle, and the big closing. Try to develop an opening for your act that works every night. Once your first laugh with a crowd happens, they and you will relax a bit. I like to use my best joke as an opener. I like to use my second best joke as my closer. Your third best joke follows the opener. Your fourth best joke leads to your closer. And so on.

All jokes have three parts, in this order: premise, set-up, punch line. The premise is the subject you're talking about; the setup is the statement that raises the crowd's anticipation; the punch line is the payoff... the funny part. (Stop talking after your punch line! Leave time for your crowd to laugh. The third time you talk over the crowd's laughter, they learn to stop laughing. Now, you don't want them to learn that, do you?) Learn this trick and other comics will give you jobs.

Always try to let your crowd focus on *you*. Maintain eye contact with your crowd. When you are onstage, don't take the microphone out of the stand unless you have some material that requires it. Stay center stage, stand and deliver. When you get steady middle act work, then explore other parts of the stage. Never, ever stroll around aimlessly! Only move around the stage if you have a quite specific reason to do so. It takes real courage to stand your ground. Only wussies pace around the stand-up stage.

When you are onstage, keep a constant eye on your elapsed time. If you've done what you think is five minutes of material, and it's been seven minutes, you are getting laughs. If it's only been three minutes when you think it's five, hey, they ain't buying it! Skip to more reliable stuff, and talk slower. You do your time and get off with the best laugh available. Do your allotted time. No more time, no less time! Learn this easy trick and then bookers will take your calls.

Build your act with five minute TV style modules. Then stack them until you reach the fifteen minute requirement for MC-ing opening acts; then thirty minutes for feature acts; and finally, fifty-five minutes to close the show. If TV happens to call, not only will these five minute modules be useable, they will be ready because you will have practiced them so frequently. This will also piss off your loved ones and friends! But, it's worth it.

Beginners will go through plateaus approximately every thirty shows. Your first thirty shows will teach you what not to do. The next thirty shows should teach you when to do what routine or bit. The next thirty shows teach you how to get jobs. The next thirty shows teach you how not to bomb. And so on. (See, there's a pattern here.)

There, that's what I know that you don't. Ten basic items. If you want the next ten items, e-mail me.

Look, I've got far more important things to do than teach you how to take jobs from me, go away! Now, go hacky sack or something . . . you're starting to bother me.

Standup comedy emanates from an oral tradition. Many tried to teach me. This meager attempt is trying to achieve a modern equivalent, gratis The Comic in Red Shoes, Lue Deck. Everybody say: **"Bye Lue!"**

Lesson seven: Assume command of the crowd right away, before it takes command of you!

The Last Honest Booking Agent!

When one prostitutes oneself for laughs, i.e. taking money to perform in a plethora of cities and states and countries, face it, most stand-up comics really need a pimp they can trust!

I've been dispatched to hundreds and hundreds of locations to do shows: nightclubs, colleges, military bases, riverboats, prisons, cruise ships, football stadiums, mansions, theaters, mud wrestling pits, and even stranger events. The one common denominator amongst them all is that almost always, it was a booking agent that arranged and/or ordered for me to go there. (Ordered because I wouldn't have gone to those places otherwise.)

As with all of the performing arts, most stand-up comics can improve only by getting endless practice. A cooperative booking agent is pretty much the best way to get enough shows to better one's act, and thereby better one's paycheck. No one agent, or agency, covers the whole country. Booking agents usually function regionally, in sort of a "This right here is **my** turf here…That's yours...over there!" verbal arrangement.

As a comic graduates from doing once or twice a week shows in his home city, he has to prove his mettle to regional and one nighter bookers. This eligibility is usually earned with a recommendation from a fellow comic, hence the saying: "Be NICE to those around you on the way UP, because, on the way DOWN, you just won't have any time!"

I've visited many bookers' offices from coast to coast, and have seen bookshelf after bookshelf full of un-viewed audition videos. (I first predicted that watching too many comic audition tapes causes tumors!)

These days, only a few bookers still go to clubs to see new performers, or create some buzz on the comedy trail to get you new jobs, or elevation in show rank. To put together a decent length tour, a stand-up has to "make his bones" with a number of bookers. Done correctly, a comic can proceed from region to region, booker to booker, and avoid those mind-bending fourteen hour drives. (And weeks off with no pay.) These iffy talent merchants are the only lifeline a comic has, as they travel around each of the booker's various circuits.

Primarily, since real contracts are few and far between, a booking agent calls, (or you phone them) to tell you where you'll perform, when, where your hotel is, and how much you'll be paid. Some booking agents, when you need them, are unreachable, undependable, and crotchety. But, there is this one guy….

The last honest booking agent works out of a sweetheart of a city: Louisville, Kentucky. (Properly pronounced: Loo-ah-vul) Tom Sobel owned and operated his own full week club, The Comedy Caravan, and produces a string of one nighter shows. His agency also books endless private events, and manages a small, select group of comics. (Lucky bastards.) He's the agent of record for a number of other full week clubs. Tom's done these harrowing chores for more than 30 years. It has cost him his hair and waistline, but he knows that's a small price to pay for the esteem in which he's held, and the respect he has earned for years. (Very little hair now and the opposite for waistline)

Having booked zillions of gigs in his illustrious career, Sobel has also put more comics on the road than Flo Ziegfeld (an old-timey booker) ever did! If you want to put on a comedy show within one day's drive of Louisville, just call TSM Artists. Tom's standup comics have done great shows in many places where comedy shows weren't really meant to be done. (The above-mentioned prisons and river boats.) The Caravan shows aboard The Star of Louisville, sailing the Ohio River, resulting in no injuries, no arrests, and no bad vibes, unlike with certain NFL players I won't mention. The trick to it all: stringing enough good shows together to make it profitable for everybody involved. Many times Tom's fee is excluded to make sure the deal is right. Hundreds of comics have achieved their "Roads Scholar" degree driving in, and out of Louisville. Caravan comics relate a continuing gag about finding numerous interstate freeway signs that read: **Food-Gas-Lodging-SOBEL GIG: 22 miles**

Some of the most nefarious bookers often give a ballpark figure about your pay, and then typically remit a lower amount. Other more suspect agents "double dip"-which means they collect a fee from the producers of a particular show, and also charge a booking fee to the funny guys. This practice is against the law in many states, but even asking if a certain show qualifies will often cost a comic that job. If an act happens to sell T-shirts or a CD after their shows, a percentage of those sales may be charged to that act, unknowingly. The quite honorable Mr. Sobel and TSM Artists have always shunned these cheap, tawdry methods, and I believe he and they always will. "Ahhhhhhhhh...Lue. We don't operate that way at TSM."

Operating as a great talent agent amounts to a 60-hour week, and its beaucoup pressure. (That's lots!) Tom is addicted to the telephone. This means that his usual day has 40 or 50 return calls. All of this madness begets problems to be solved. *(Where can you get a new Microphone...and a Honda carburetor on I-65? Tom knows. What do you do when a hotel washing machine turns all your clothes pink??...Sobel said to go to Kmart. The club I'm performing at has burned down, the motel won't give me a room, and what do I do??...Tom says to drive to the next town, another Caravan gig, go to the comic's condo, your opener last week is working there this week, and he'll let you in! (...that* Sobel must be a God!)

Problems are right in his wheelhouse. He does problems! But, for all his facility in staging live shows ... anywhere, Mr. Sobel has his idiosyncrasies too. He likes to talk. He likes to eat! This man knows the best places to eat in fourteen states, and he'll tell you about it. Then, he'll tell you that he told you about it!

Despite massive computer backup, Tom Sobel, like most of the better agents, keeps it all in his head, and he'll tell you about it. Many times, he and I have left his club during a weekend show to drive around and check out some other club's parking lots, comparing customer activity. Those whirling dervishes in the mid-east have nothing on Sobel's non-stop days, and nights, and he'll tell you about it.

This jolly prevaricator of cash for laughs has also loaned, or donated huge piles of money to needy comics. But, he won't tell you about that. Tom's really a working act's best friend. This talkative Friar Tuck has pissed away uncountable sums taking care of comics, and the problems they encounter on tour every damn day. Enough to moolah buy Masada! (Which I heard he has inspected.)

I salute this impresario who orchestrated, and cast his own Showtime special with his own great acts. (Even though I wasn't one of them, damnit! He sent me to Palm Beach.)

I raise my glass of Three Stooges Beer to the booker who can get a Western Union Money-gram to an interstate freeway rest stop, to rescue a damn prop act!

Kudos to the man who once escorted the legendary and quite tipsy Ollie Joe Prater from a Bourbon Street Comedy Club green room back to the ten blocks distant hotel…in a baggage cart. (And gave a nice tip!)

Now, listening to the final strains of The Curley Shuffle, as I hop aboard my Camel and ride into the sunset, heading for the next in a series of endless one-nighters, I just wanted to tell that tall, balding guy with seven weeks of straight work, and more friends than he will ever realize: Ahhhhhhhhhhhhhhhhhh… Thanks Tom!

Closing this paean to a passing breed, I quote Robert Frost: "HOME is where you go, and they HAVE TO take you in!"

If you are in search of stand-up comedy being done, the way it should be done, call Louisville! Call now! The Comedy Caravan and Tom Sobel will take you in…and make you feel at home! He might just be the last, honest booking agent!

Lesson eight: Improvisers say: "Give up focus to get it back!" Give up what you want, so you can get it back. Verbal space is always appreciated.

As you enter the stage, project your own happiness at meeting your new best friends. When you're the MC/opener, the pressure on you is to make the club owner or booker feel good, without pissing off the other acts, or the crowd. Make all of your show announcements happily, learn the other acts introduction thoroughly and quickly, and get off stage on time! These efforts will get you re-booked!

LUE DECK

The Greatest Star That Never Was!

(Ollie Joe Prater, a Saga with No Regrets)

There never was a stand-up that didn't fail. There never was a comic with such ardent and loyal fans. Never was there a comedy act that ransacked his audiences with such laughs, woops, snorts, and guffaws like him. And, if there had been, no one would believe it. But, there was!

I know there was such a comic! I was his opening act, touring partner, and his fellow road warrior. I watched it all happen for seventeen years. I'm honor-bound and compelled to tell you about the stand-up comic Richard Pryor aptly referred to as: "The Renegade White Man." I want to tell you about the greatest star that never was: Ollie Joe Prater.

A 390 pound, five-foot-five, bearded and mustachioed, cowboy-booted varmint swaggers onstage, grabs the microphone and roars: *"I'm an educated man!"* He then sticks a long neck beer down his gullet, manages to finish it in three gulps (with no hands!) then spits the bottle on the floor. With a satisfied and very proud gasp, Ollie Joe Prater would then bellow: *"That there's everything I learned in college!"*

In what is now deemed the Golden Age of stand-up comedy in LA, Ollie Joe found his way to the world famous Comedy Store. By hook, and flash, or crook, OJ was made manager of the Westwood Comedy Store, the first satellite of the original on Sunset Blvd. in 1974. OJ gave me my first job in show biz in 1975. At the Comedy Store in the 70's and 80's, you would rub elbows with the likes of Richard Pryor, Johnny Carson, David Letterman, Jay Leno, Arsenio Hall, Andy Kauffman, Gallagher, and countless others soon-to-be big names.(Even Bat Man!) The Comedy Store was a showcase club, where you honed your stand-up act for TV shows. TV bookers expected a laugh every twenty seconds, called LPMs. (Laughs per minute.) An act that was well known enough, and sharp enough, might well graduate from LA's staircase system to open for big stars like Frank Sinatra, Aretha Franklin, Wayne Newton, Patty LaBelle and other such money-makers. Stars were born, some shined brightly, and some even went super nova. It was an exciting time and place. Audacity was in the air!

In 1981, at the world's first full week, three act comedy club, the Comedy Store (La Jolla) OJ recorded his first comedy album: "The Renegade White Man."Ollie Joe's LPM rate was five, which was very fast. Having reputation for borrowing material had brought phone calls from other comics wishing their particular jokes good luck. Paul Mooney and Vic Dunlap were among the first. OJ readily admitted to stealing some primo jokes. He tried to cultivate other comic's fear as a social equalizer, so they'd be scared of him and treat him with more respect. And that's probably the best place to leave that. Ollie's album was sold only through the Comedy Store, and no record of any sales was kept. We can only guess at the thousands of copies sold, it might have amounted to a minor league record of some kind. We just don't know.

In 1982, character-comic types were big in film, cable TV and the three broadcast networks. So, our Comedy Store team put together some modest efforts as our queen (read here: Mitzi!) made a deal with ABC to feature a joke-driven production named "Buckshot!" Ollie Joe Prater, a gruff, stout cowboy-type, got as many of his jokes in as the political satirists did. OJ even got to do special guest spots on the Bert Convey show. Look it up. Wikipedia is completely wrong, again!

After the Comedy Store's illustrious owner, Mitzi Shore, politely invited him to try his act on tour, Ollie Joe left that safe haven in October 1982. He tested himself with the real audiences across our country. Not all performers can count on their jokes and routines that worked in Hollywood. Adjustments for different regions, age groups, and income-brackets were required. Some acts did well in the South, some in the Midwest and others in the North. Only a rare few succeeded all over. Ollie Joe learned to adjust to his crowd, instead of mistakenly expecting the crowds to adjust to him. This was a key ingredient to becoming America's most powerful stand-up comic. A booking agent with the most consistent and well-paying circuits in the known comedy world, Tom Sobel of Louisville KY, described Ollie Joe as the real life embodiment of "Yosemite Sam" the high energy cartoon character of Looney Tunes fame. And Mr. Sobel was "darned tootin' right!" Ollie Joe often called Mr. Sobel "The last honest booking agent!" Sobel's execution of OJ's "Get out of MY Way!" video in 1986 proves the point elegantly. Tom even got comic/singer James Lee Reeves to compose a catchy theme song for Ollie Joe.

Before most cities had a comedy club, stand-up shows were mostly one-nighters. Do your shows, get paid, and then move on to the next town; that was the insane life a working comic woke to daily. Deal with it! Being loud, fast-paced and crazy-funny was quite valuable to most bookers. OJ was that, and much, much more! Soon enough, Ollie's dance card starting filling up. As gigs that had shows all week began cropping up, a good, strong act didn't have to travel daily. Stand-up life was getting even better! OJ understood that he was a big club favorite, and calculated he could perform in each of his most profitable cities at least three times a year, get stronger on stage, and be handsomely paid forever. Stand-up life was great! 1985 proved his endless maneuvers correct. By 1987, Ollie Joe and I were appearing in 80 cities every year. The one-nighters were harder to do, but paid so well, we (read here OJ) couldn't refuse most offers.

Homer, Michigan's biggest celebrity never forgot his roots. OJ visited home regularly, to do free benefit shows for the local fire departments. They cheered him on like a native son. After winning Showtime's "Funniest!" in Texas, Ollie Joe quickly realized that his straight-forward and blunt language act would have little future on television for the time being. So he restricted himself to live shows. Let the bland TV acts come compete for heavy dollars on the road, with real folks doing the real laughing. Or, the not laughing. It was brutal on the weaker acts we knew. OJ knew he would dominate almost all of the comics that didn't have his hard-to-get know how. That group included most headliners, even the famous ones. What an education we all got!

Ollie Joe claimed not to understand gay men: *"Outside every men's shower and men's room, there should be a big damn sign. Picture of a man's private, big red circle around it, with a slash all the way though!* **If it ain't your dick, then don't touch it!**!

We got, as Ollie Joe liked to say: "All scientific on their asses!" He had bought audio and video recorders to study what we were doing in all these weird places. I taped most of our shows, and we would watch and talk about how we could get better. That was Ollie Joe's passion, getting better…being a better comic than you were last year. And lo and behold: we shaped our shows and got better. It was like one of those damn metaphors! If our Comedy Store years were like Comedy College, then touring constantly for seven straight years is like getting your Master's degree and Ph.D. in the art of stand-up comedy. An old vaudeville saw claims if a comic can get any moisture out of his crowd, he killed them. Any moisture basically means: crying, snorting, flatulence, snot, spit, or pee. Ollie Joe Prater could make his happiest crowds spit up and choke with laughter. I asked him how he did it. OJ claimed he didn't know himself. It took me watching his every show for two years to isolate his technique. After twenty-five minutes onstage, Ollie worked his LPM rate to three per minute for ten straight minutes, then switched to adult jokes, pause and delay his punch lines until he could tell the crowd was breathing together, then speed up his LPMs to six per minute. The change in breathing with tempo usually made the biggest laughers out there choke and spit up. Many of the rest would be pleased at this and applaud. It was quite a lesson.

Now, stand-up life was magnificent! Ollie asked me where we should go on tour. I told him: "Let's do half new places and the other half, just our favorite ones!" At the time, it was one of the best years we ever had. But, Ollie Joe knew it could get better. And he was right. Ollie and I performed in clubs, auditoriums, mud wrestling pits, strip joints, concert halls, buses, limos, airplanes, TV and radio studios, funeral parlors, caves, boats (Cruise ships, steamers, tug boats, house boats, barges, river boats) and there were even stranger places. Believe it or not, this wild and wooly dynamo would quote existential philosophers to me. "Say, boy… (I'm 32 and six feet four, dammit! How big to I have to get before you quit calling me boy?)…"Say, boy…as my opening act, what doesn't destroy you, makes ME stronger! If you eat it out there, I won't! Get it? I'm watching ya! If you die, then I don't have to! That's why I pay you! Get out there, go get 'em! I'll be watchin' ya!" We did shows in big and small prisons, jails, baseball and football stadiums, RV's, caverns, country clubs, barns, churches, bars, offices, factories, lodges, anyplace that would pay us sufficiently. And not one time did I ever see Ollie Joe tank a show, or have a bad show, or bomb out a room. Not even once! It wasn't like that for me. I ate the big one many times, but my first job was to set the stage for OJ. When he saw me die a horrible stand-up death opening for him, he would make his adjustments to win the crowd over. Ollie Joe never gave up on a crowd. It was like watching a brain surgeon work his voodoo.

Once, after driving for five hours, Ollie Joe had an unusual epiphany, one rainy night in Georgia. (I know! But, it's OJ's joke!) "Say boy…differnce twixt you and me is I'm talented! and you ain't! (He wasn't joking!) You're skilled with words…now me, I talk my ideas. It works fine for me! But, you, you try to figure out ahead whatever it is these particular folks will laugh at…you should try it my way!" I told him he should try it mine. It really was a rainy night in Georgia, (I swear!) We were very bored and feeling unimportant. (It **was** Georgia) So, we made a small bet, (hah!) and the game was on. I sucked on stage for three shows; OJ looked like he'd found a new toy! Before the fourth show, Ollie took me aside and told me I should revert back to my old style because I was certainly no Renegade White Man. I felt like I had gotten a reprieve from ad-lib hell. Back to my sacred notes. I kicked ass for the next two weeks, but I noticed Ollie Joe had kinda changed. We started going straight back to our hotel right after our shows. "Work them damn tapes!" OJ kept repeating. "None of that drinking and partying tonight! We're going back to study our acts and write some new jokes." Suddenly, Ollie Joe's phone wouldn't stop ringing. It seemed like there was a line forming to book our open dates. It was 1988; uniquely, we had the entire year booked by January. "C'mon boy…lets you and me go tell some jokes!" And we did. We ended working 108 cities that year. Stand up life was glorious! I'll never know if I was banging the drum slowly for Ollie Joe, or if he was banging the drum slowly for me.

Then one day, Ollie Joe sent me away. Although his hard-hitting, harsh-language act never failed, Ollie Joe's health finally did. The years of travel, signature weight problem, booze, cocaine, and just plain hard living took its toll. As he realized he was dying, he booked an eight week tour for me, while he rested. In Barbados, six weeks later, I got a call from a sergeant with the Tampa Police telling me that Ollie Joe had died. When I spoke with OJ's sister, she told me they wanted all the attention directed at their local boy from Homer, MI. Not the flamboyant character he created. I agreed with his family then. But now, I have to say a little something for this mostly unsung Comedy Store graduate magna cum loudly. First, Ollie Joe would love the mistakes and lies about him on Wikipedia. He knew his critics and detractors didn't know the truth. He thought it was funny, just how wrong they were about him and his doings.

Ollie Joe knew how to leave his crowd laughing. *"I know that one out of every three people in this world is UGLY! Look to your left; now look to your right! If ya don't see ugly, guess what?* **It must be you!** *Nice seats buddy!"*

I watched every act at The Comedy Store for nine years. Figuring in LPMs and thousands of live shows, I know in my heart that Ollie Joe Prater was the best stand-up comic I ever saw. This includes everybody, even Robin Williams and Richard Pryor. But his real self, Gilbert Hartzog, was even more. To go from where Gilbert came from, all the way to where Ollie Joe ended up, was a mind boggling journey that encompassed light years of scrapping and learning. And before he quit this good earth, he knew who he was, and what he accomplished. You can search online: The Renegade White Man. I really just wanted you to know a little more about my partner, and my best friend. In my very humblest of opinions, Ollie Joe Prater will always be **THE GREATEST STAR THAT NEVER WAS!** Rest in peace, big fella!

Lesson nine: Make a dignified, quick exit. (From the time you tell your crowd good night, you should be out of their sight and unable to draw any visual focus in 5 to 7 seconds, because the show must go on! (Smile, you want the crowd to see and realize that you both just had a great time!)

Jokes or Attitude?

When you are laughing with a stand-up comedian, it may not make much difference to you whether the comic is a joke guy or an attitude guy. But for those on the way up the showbiz staircase, it could be the deciding factor between a three year career, and a great gig that may last decades.

At this point, it's fair to say that all comics tell jokes, and all comics usually have some type of an attitude. The telling sign is what each use to keep their momentum going with a crowd. The real key to a comic's durability is likeability. Face it, if the crowd doesn't like you, it won't matter what style you use.

In the interest of full disclosure, I freely admit I am a joke comic. I never asked to be rich and famous, and funny enough, things have worked out that way. My stand-up career has spanned some 34 years. It has clothed me, it has fed me, and it has joked me around this old planet three times, so I have no complaints.

What is a joke comic? What is an attitude comic? The differences between each are vast, as vast as the differences between a fastball guy and a curveball guy in baseball. Contemporary examples can compare and contrast to help make each style more apparent.

Attitudes and jokes are the yin and yang of stand-up performance. Joke comics tell jokes. Well, what is a joke? A joke is a short, declarative statement, surprising with a funny twist at the end, and elicits laughter. Have you heard the late-night comics talk about our president? Their short statements are usually jokes.

Have you ever heard Jon Stewart do the same? With all his facial mugging and clever smirks, he proves he is an attitude comic. Oh, Mr. Stewart tells a lot of jokes, but mostly, it's his attitude that pulls in all his laughter. ABC's Jimmy Kimmel uses virtually the same technique, but his writers are simply not as skilled as Mr. Stewart's! Remember Emo Phillips? Emo's attitude was *so dorky*, we couldn't help but laugh at his weird antics. Do you remember Sam Kennison or Andrew "Dice" Clay? I knew both very well, and lived in Mitzi's Comedy Store house with them. I watched as each willingly chose to perform an attitude act, instead of learning to tell jokes. Their stand-up careers are over now because of those choices.

Remember Elayne Boozler? Brassy and blond, Elayne was the best female joke teller I've ever seen. She still makes a nice living some thirty years later. I cite Jerry Seinfeld, who's the finest joke technician in stand-up history. His joke skill gave him unimaginable riches in live and situational comedy on TV.

Comparing Jay Leno and The Tonight Show to Dave Letterman and The Late Show showcases some vital differences between joke tellers and attitude pullers. Jay Leno is undisputedly the best at telling jokes since Johnny Carson relinquished the crown. In Mr. Carson's tradition, Jay hired some of the best joke-writers on the planet and his opening monologues show it. (Unless it's Friday) Jay even finds jokes in reality with his *Headlines* routine.

Whereas Dave plays the same opening gambit, it's just a matter of time until he repeats a punch line for effect, which is the classic move attitude guys use to maintain the audience's attention on said attitude. Also, *Will It Float?* as a routine does not contain any jokes what so-ever. But it is funny! And that *funniness is entirely due to* Letterman's attitude that this bit (Will if float or not?) should be taken absolutely seriously.

Attitude comics can't shift their attitude to reality, they manage to shift reality to their attitude. It's my opinion that although audiences may accept certain abrasive attitudes for a while, they will eternally laugh at good jokes. An attitude comic may bitch about our current president, but joke comics will always make you laugh with truth and supposition, as in the following:

The one thing I like about President George Bush Jr. is that he has a worse arrest record than I do!

There are three Howdy Doodys in existence. One is on display in The Smithsonian Institute, the second is owned by the heirs of his partner, Buffalo Bob. The third is retired from The White House and living in Dallas, TX.

Did you hear that Bush Jr. had his third colonoscopy? All the doctors found was an impression of his own head!

No matter which style of comedian you follow, the one important fact that carries the day is: "Laughter is the vital oil that keeps the gears in the human machine from grinding down our souls!" If you feel down, or have the blues, a visit to your local comedy club can work wonders.

Lesson ten: Review your last show. Compare your set list to your audio to see where and when you left your advance plan. Why? Which jokes did not work? Which jokes worked? This is how you build your first five minute set.

The Night nothing was funny!

The pieces came careening at me like a cosmic puzzle. I hadn't realized it yet, but I was walking into a stand-up comic's nightmare!

I had just come from the finest comedy club in America, The Comedy Caravan in Louisville, KY (Great money, six days work, nice stage, decent housing, and friends). Happily, I began the next week's work on a tour of twelve different cities in two weeks. If you can't do the "A" clubs, one-nighters (long drives, cheap or no motels, bad stages, and some venue managers reluctant to pay) are the easiest shows for most comics to book. As the particular establishment in question is still open, with nasty lawyers, I decline to mention the name of the business, or the city. The truth is, if I made fun of him and he caught up with me, a certain humongous bouncer promised to erase my scrawny butt from the planet. I write this with the safety that he's certainly not an Internet user, because he probably still can't read.

The first piece of the puzzle worked its way into the picture unobtrusively. The rat of a booking agent told me the names of the other two acts. They were from Detroit and I didn't know them. That was only the first of many red flags that I would miss. My quasi-official world record for performing in 1000 cities in ten years had left me with an idea of most of the knuckleheads, who, like me, were crisscrossing America.

I'm a LA comic. I hoped they spoke the same stand-up language as me.

The next two puzzle pieces cartwheeled past me like a horny cheerleader. My itinerary revealed the show that night was at 7pm, and was at the same address as our accommodations. This is never a good sign for a tour like this. Doing a comedy show at 7pm? It's my experience that a drinking crowd is at its most uncontrollable either very late or very early…a 7pm show?? Also, when you do a show in the same place as you stay, everybody knows in which rooms of the motel the comics stay. Hope you like visitors!

After I checked in with the motel, they told me I would be in the Pat Paulsen room. No big deal, he was the act appearing last week, so I got the same room.

The fourth piece of the puzzle slapped me in the face as I walked into the adjacent bar to inspect the stage. There was a brass pole on the stage, and I now knew there was going to be trouble at the show tonight. If you don't get it yet, brass poles mean there are strippers nearby. Strippers?? That's not good for Mr. Jokey-boy! It's especially not good for Mr. Jokey-boy, if he wears Red Shoes.

I wandered back to my room to see if the other acts had checked in yet. Nope! I found the washing machines and dryers and washed everything I owned. When one is on the road, one doesn't know when one can wash their show clothes and daily wear next. I thought I was just staying ahead of the curve. When I came to change my stuff into the dryer; I just about had a hissy fit. Everything I owned was a cute, light pink! Another piece of my crazy puzzle fit into its place. Frantically, I dashed off to buy new clothes for the show. I'll never curse K-Mart again. I found some. A thought hit me: "Why is this night different from every other night?" I went back to my room and found phone messages from the other two acts. A Miss Gwen Sarrong and the other was from Peter and Billy. I returned the calls. Now, thirty minutes before the show began, I was informed my opening act was a transvestite, and my closing act was a ventriloquist! His dummy told me not to do any cat jokes, and the transvestite warned me not to wear my Red Shoes. Exactly why I do not take ventriloquists seriously, much less some guy in drag singing.

I went to the showroom early to check in with the venue manager and discovered the audience was primarily from some lumberjack outfit, with some stragglers streaming in from the local slaughterhouse. Not counting the strippers, there wasn't a woman in the house. I was sure all the pieces of my ambush puzzle had fallen into place, and then I saw the headline stripper start a backstage catfight with our visiting trans-gender type person. Great…Gypsy Rose Lee vs. Betty Boop on steroids.

I stepped between the scantily clad combatants and reminded Diana, or Larry, or Miss Whoosis, the comedy show started in ten minutes. To this day, I'm not sure which of them left that powder handprint on the seat of my new pants. But they separated and we each went to our various dressing areas. Mine was the janitor's closet, which was OK, because the smell prevented any visitors from popping in. I checked to see if I was still presentable, and wandered out to judge my opener's competency. The slaughterhouse guys weren't buying it, and they weren't laughing. The lumberjacks offered to do a sex change operation right there using their axes!

But, they were joshing and in a good mood, so I steeled myself for an interactive show. At the 10 minute mark, he/she/it started crying and rushed from the stage. Maybe his multi-sequined gown with the plunging back was just pinching too tight. I prayed for luck and marched to center stage. I announced there would be a raffle to find out who got to drive the stripper home, after she beat the crap out of Diana! This seemed to please the meat packers and lumberjacks, as well as the guy who had to pay me. Hardly a killer start, but I had everybody going!

Next, I told them I was Lue Deck, The Comic in Red Shoes, and I'd skin any dude here who believed I was a sissy like Diana/Larry! More laughs from the cheap seats. Hell, there was nothing but cheap seats in this place. I did best my sex and pot jokes, hoping that would fit the mood. It did! More big laughs. On a roll, I left the stage with a cordless microphone and started plowing my way through the now seventy or so souls in attendance. I did the old "play the crowd trick" asking individuals questions and lampooning their answers. I insulted every guy in the place, and they thought it was pretty cool.

Actually, I must've gone a little too far while laying into one heckler. He was the bouncer, and son of the owner who was dating the pugilistic stripper. I told the crowd I had seen him slipping out of the cross dresser's bedroom before the show. This young moron pulled a knife and offered to end my miserable existence…now. His raucous buddies restrained him long enough for the manager to approach the stage and pay me, while he advised me the hot-head would bust loose soon. I took my bow, smiled and went back to my room.

I packed, checked out, jumped in my car and headed towards the next town. Welcome to the comedy trail, where just about anything can happen. Oh yeah, that ventriloquist…I heard later…the crowd tried to lynch his dummy.

I smiled again, knowing I had barely survived the night when nothin' was funny!

Lesson eleven: Record your show and listen to it five times before going onstage again. Record your next twenty shows. This will help you to make better choices for your next five minute set. To get your first job doing stand-up, you'll need a series of five minute sets.

Hell's Cruise Ship!

If you can force your Freud, Jung, and Dr. Phil back in their respective closets for a moment, I've got a story to tell you. If you can't, just ignore me and go invade another country.

Mythologies supporting after-death events have peppered mankind's recorded history. My contention here is that certain lost souls, after departing their personal judgment, exit quickly, straight downward, on the Hades Express. (Perhaps you've heard the phrase: Go straight to hell!)

After all disembark from the Hades Express, funny enough, there's **NO Smoking!**

Then, a sorting process begins. This process was adopted from Germany's Nazis, and as a result, the Nazis reap the very worst treatment. It's only logical that the more hateful you behaved during your life, the more you will suffer in your after-life. However, logic doesn't include teasing, irony, or sarcasm. Guess what? Hell surely does, and there's a surprise for everybody!

Murderers, pedophiles, dictators and the like belong in certain groups with the appropriate punishments. Tax accountants, lawyers, and baseball umpires will merit special treatment.

War profiteers, and embezzlers, and Don King all belong in the correct, painful places. But, one special place in hell that you may not have heard of is Hell's Cruise Ship! I foresee this as kind of like Carnival cruises on a really, really bad week.

The parameters that mandate an individual's selection to sail on this wicked boat are limited, while at the same time, quite broad. Only a few are listed here, so watch your sorry asses!

Have you ever fixed, or help fix the election? Have you ever kicked a kitty or a puppy? Ever yell at a busboy or waitress? Ever scalped tickets? Ever used the "N" word? How about grease-painting your body to attend a sporting event? Ever buy a rap CD and hit someone with it? Ever drive 2 miles an hour under the posted limit… in the fast lane? Have you ever wasted a busy doctor's time? Have you ever denied a veteran due medical coverage? Have you needlessly been unkind to your fellow man?

If you have, the Prince of Darkness has a cabin, reserved for you!

The devil ship is the Bismarck redoux. The Bismarck's itinerary includes two kinds of voyages. The first, standard visits to places that nobody would ever want to go. One trip included stopping at Pompeii 20 seconds before the volcano erupted. The next stop was a German concentration camp in 1943, followed by porting in Nagasaki Japan, just two seconds after the atomic blast hit. Then, on to Joan Rivers last episode of plastic surgery. Beelzebub's object in this trip is to help his passengers understand that a living hell on earth is still better than their living hell, in Hell!

The second type of voyage usually includes all manner of glorious destinations, like Jamaica, or Hawaii, or the jet-set spots of the Mediterranean Sea. But, on these trips, none of his passengers will be allowed to leave the ship… Ever. The Devils lesson here would be to display and deny all kinds of heavens on earth to those consigned on board. Gee, that rascal Scratch is diabolical and evidently… he's a real prick, too.

To prove that fact, Mephistopheles has arranged for all the voyages to be upside down, for maximum discomfort. The higher up your cabin is, the further underwater you will be. Bottoms up!

As far as activities on board, the bars are open, and the shops are open, and the casino is open, but whoops, none of the doomed has any money. It's just not fair! The one and only diversion is mandatory attendance at the dinner shows in the main theater, nightly. Better be there… Lucifer is not joking!

There's a quintuplet of really bad ventriloquists hosting the dinner show. These psycho-babble rejects seem to think their role is to totally alienate all of the audience, much like in real life. The River Styx Orchestra is actually radio DJs faking hokey movement to music playback. Stars of the shows are comics, who don't know that if anyone laughs even once, the laugher will immediately be ejected from the ship to share the Nazi sector. (And you know how much they hate that.) Now, you can truly see, a good time cannot be had by all, or anyone here! Such is the heart and mind of the Supreme Spirit of Evil.

Oh, El Diablo's tortured show has seen lots of familiar names. Many comics are scheduled here for various comeuppances. Fatty Arbuckle, that goofball, was the headliner here, seems like for an eternity. Cut up Lenny Bruce just ruled the place until recently. Sam Kennison toiled here for weeks, until he kept infuriating our all-seeing owner with Jesus jokes, over and over. Sam works in the engine room now. There are no women there. There's a place saved for him next for Andrew "Dice" Clay. Same sins.

But, you really should watch the second act. No matter what they look like… I'll tell you the secret: the second act is always God! Yeah, it's God! It's hard to believe that someone that high up the ladder could be so funny. It's hard not to laugh. Very hard… not to laugh. But, you know **whom**, is always watching. The truth is, when the boss is away doing his "steal your soul" bit, some of us actually do laugh at God's newest jokes. That God is "fall down" funny! If anyone in the crowd laughs, they're zapped away to the nasty Hitler's zone. But, unknown to the Arch-fiend, moments later, those who laughed, got immediate clemency in the form of redemption.

The most doomed of all doomed present are the comics who go on stage next. Remember, these who have to follow God's act, don't know the crowd's deal with the dark Angel. Now, that's the constant insidiousness this of comedy hell.

Those standup comics appearing next have obviously sinned against their peers during their wretched careers. Sinned by continuing various amateur and hack behaviors, and littering stages across their performing lives. Now, on this their final home stage, these boorish stand-ups reap what they have sown, for all time. It's all courtesy of the Lord of the Underworld, the shadowy one who wears the black jersey numbered: **666!**

A warning to those who still walk the earth: beware of unkindness, love one another, and **do good** and be just, or you too may sail for the rest of time…… On Hell's cruise ship!

Lesson twelve: Always offer to open any show. Offer to MC any show. Get a positive looking headshot. (Sometimes, that's what gets you the work.) Get a positive looking resume. (Sometimes, that's why they take your phone calls.) Demo tape your act on YouTube.

If I were King!

We've all thought it. Thinking about it doesn't do any harm. I'm not sure about you, but I'd make a whole lot of changes. Oh, the changes you and I would make, if only we were King of the World!

Now, don't get hinky on me. I've thought it out. As King of the World, when I'm done with these five obvious changes, I'll resign. Or, you can shoot me and reorganize the government on **your** Plan B. Same-same.

First: I will unveil my newest discovery. It's a sub-atomic particle process I call The Nanno-Stopper. It slows molecular flow like a duck in molasses, preventing the vital chain reaction. When activated, The Nanno-stopper renders all nuclear weapons on Earth completely **unworkable.** This will stop all of us from blowing up our planet! At the same time, it will completely piss off anyone who has nukes. The funny part is: It's actually fueled by Soy Sauce.

The bad news is now everything will smell like Chinese food for a while.

Second: There will be a law insisting individuals learn to how read as a condition for getting food. To get better food, you'd have to graduate from middle school. To get some Chocolate goodies, you would have to learn to use a computer. To get wine, beer, or booze, it'll take enrollment in college. To smoke cigarettes, or use a Jacuzzi, you'll have to graduate. Vote, and Do Jury Duty, you get free bananas for life. Read two hundred books: Now, you can own a car. WRITE a book, get a free trip to Las Vegas. (That's true now.) Complete your Master's Degree, you'll be allowed to exceed the speed limit by 30 mph, forever! Those folks who educate themselves will **always** be able to do more than those who don't.

Third: **ALL** ventriloquists, mimes, and impressionists are really **twisted** souls. So they will be forced to perform for each other only, for the rest of all eternity.

Fourth: Let's do good, exactly **where** good needs to be done. Let's start by building a lot of pharmaceutical factories in African nations to make and distribute AIDS drugs to patients free and faster. Order Merck, Pfizer, Lily, and all the other rich pill boys to drag their butts and go help where they are needed most. Along this line of thinking, I'll also move The Crest and Oral B companies into Great Britain. The Hooked on Phonics people will take over all Canada. I will order the rock band REM to do a gnarly concert in Tallinn, Estonia. Listerine, Right Guard, and Nair will open massive factories in France! Aerial spraying of Valium and Prozac commences over the entire Middle East.

Fifth: Everybody on the planet gets their own pair of Nikes, and a large helium balloon! 'Leggo Land' will invent the five-person, low-cost house. It would cost a mere $1000. It's red, yellow, and blue. Before 2010, we will export ten million worldwide, except in flood zones, tornado zones, or The Republic of Santa Monica. Lastly, no one will be allowed to sing We Are the World, in public, ever again.

That's all; revoke the ventriloquist thingy if it's too harsh or too personal to me. I resign! Effective immediately, I am no longer your king. Good luck to the next guy in line (BANG-BANG! Ha Ha, missed me!). Long live The New King!

Lesson thirteen: You will always think you are funnier than the other acts. And they think they're funnier than you. You should find out why.

The Cop and the Comic!

(What was I thinking?)

We met on a cruise ship. No names please, but the ship was with a cruise line that rhymes with "Parnival! It was a fairy tale romance. The cynic in me should have been tipped off right away that this wasn't real!

We've all heard that old saw: *"Love is like a bird in the hand, if you hold it too tight, you'll crush it! If you hold too loosely, it will fly away! And if it does fly away, then that love was never meant to be!"* Well, when we flew away from each other, it was hard to tell which of us was the most relieved!

The Holiday ported at Cozumel, The Cayman Islands, and Ocho Rios, Jamaica. By the time we got back to Miami, I was in head over heels! It was love at first handcuffs! She wore red shoes, when we were wed.

For two years, I was happy, she wasn't. I never saw it coming. When it happened, I really didn't want to get the divorce. But the FBI guy she happened to be sleeping with…downright insisted!

I decided to step up and settle this like a man. Then I realized that she already did!

She told me right after court that day: "Don't ever get arrested. I'll hear about it, and somehow I'll be there!" So, I don't speed in my car, or even litter anymore. That reunion, I don't want to be there for.

I tell this joke about it: On the same day that I got divorced, I up, and lost my divorce papers. (Arms and legs akimbo, flailing like an epileptic) I guess it must have been sometime during the dance! (…I'm free! I'm free…)

To get to my point: I just love strong women. They are the best! My Mom was a strong woman. So was her Mom. My sister is still one of the strongest women I've ever met. She married a cop too.

I some advice for you men: If you're lucky enough to have a strong woman in your life, whether you're sitting with her, loving her, living with her, or just know that you want a strong woman…You nurture her. You listen to her. You support her and her choices or…..she will break both of your damn legs!

See, I know this. I do love strong women. In fact, the woman I was married to was a Sergeant of Police in Tampa, Florida. (Now, a Captain of Internal Affairs.) To this day, I just don't know what in God's name… what was I thinking??

Although, given the chance to have sex in her patrol car at seventy MPH on Interstate 75…No! No…Never mind! What was I thinking??

You may not believe this, but it's hard, being married to a policewoman. I bet there's not one other man reading this, that gets pistol-whipped…when he leaves that toilet seat up.

You may not believe this either, but it's hard, very hard, sleeping with a policewoman. Her gun? Hey, it was bigger than mine!

Actually, the last time we made love, she gave me a ticket…for goin' too fast!

I think what really pissed her off though…was that rear-end collision!

She tried to book me for Assault and Battery…..with a dead weapon.

I told her: "The evidence will never stand up in court!"

But, I'm a better man for the experience. I've also gained a whole new respect for those that carry a gun and badge. If you think your life is tough, try doing the right thing every moment of every day, every day of every week, and every week of every year. It gets harder to do, the further you get in! It's an awesome burden to bear, but those who protect and serve, they ask for it. They ask for that burden every day they go to work. So, if you can, cut 'em some slack, won'tcha?

And, if you happen to see, or happen to hear that I got arrested, just please, please, just don't call Tampa!

Lesson fourteen: If your joke doesn't work, it's your fault! (Never blame anyone, because you failed to find their funny bone.)

He Made Me Do It!

Since I'm not a surgeon with a scalpel, or an airline mechanic with a hangover, I think it'll be OK if I share my little secret with you: I hear these tiny voices inside my head, and they tell me what to do!

It goes back to when I was a small child. My older siblings wouldn't play with me…the bastards! So I was left to myself to keep occupied, and I found new friends, even if no one but me could see or hear them.

My first imaginary friend told stories foretelling lessons I would need to learn. I was about twelve when he told me how he came to talk so convincingly. He told me that his father insisted he do all the plowing. He asked his father why his older brother didn't have to it. His father told him his brother had talked his way out of the lousy chore, and also stuck his little brother with all the work. I never forgot that. From then on, I always tried to pick and use my words well.

One day in high school chemistry class, I fell asleep, dreaming of my first imaginary girlfriend. Rudely awakened by an architect's scale being bonked on my poor punkin' head, I was commanded to repeat the lesson that I was napping through. My invisible pal whispered to me the subject was gas, expressed in volumes, and my teacher had just said: "A common kitchen match, when lit, releases ten times its weight in fumes." Armed with this inside information, I offered a demonstration the next day for the whole class. Having hacked off the nozzle to a CO_2 cartridge, I cut the heads off two books of matches. Next, I put the match-heads in the empty cartridge with one peeking out to start the desired chain reaction. Lastly, I placed the cartridge inside a hollow tent tube to aim it. Voila! I'd invented the bazooka.

I hadn't planned to light it, so my invisible friend did. Voila! The ensuing discharge penetrated the Principal's '68 VW! Inventors are misunderstood. My imaginary pal and I had detention for two weeks.

I told the Selective Service Board about all of my imaginary friends in hopes it would help me avoid the draft. They said it didn't help much. In my life, I've had many encounters with these friendly voices. Some of these meetings have led to inevitable epiphanies; others have led me to question my already questionable sanity. Some say you aren't responsible for all the thoughts that come into your mind, just the thoughts you entertain. Well, in my head, we're having a big party!

During my tenure as a road comic, I've driven almost nine hundred thousand miles across this bumpy land, usually alone. Talk Radio always makes me so angry, I usually end up speeding. Music gets repetitive. So, imaginary friends made long hours bearable and led to lively conversations. Once, my then- current, imaginary friend advised me to vote for Ralph Nader. This example proves our imaginary folks are indeed fallible, and that they have a wicked sense of humor.

But, the one imaginary friend I will never forget is the buddy that demanded that I must become a stand-up comic. Now, as I'm further from the start of my career than the end of it, I'd like to honor that encouraging voice that spoke inside my mixed up noggin.

That voice convincing me I could make people laugh, tipped the balance for me. I hesitated when it came to doing my first stand-up show. But the little sangfroid voice kept after me, telling me that everything would be just fine. I wrangled a spot at Gilley's, the big western club in Pasadena, just outside Houston, made famous by their mechanical bull and its riders. My voice was silent about this choice. After all the cowboys rode the mechanical bull, amidst loud pizza pick-up announcements, my little voice urged me to go for it. Very few of the hundred or so folks in attendance were paying much attention, until I rushed to the stage, grabbed the microphone, and announced a line would be forming for all cowboys to RIDE the waitresses! That got some good laughs, and I was off and running with three horse jokes, (suggested by my pals) three half jokes (mine), and three obviously stolen jokes, (from Johnny Carson, Richard Pryor, and Tom Dreesen…Thanks guys!) Almost everybody laughed, except for the waitresses. Today, I know without my imaginary friends' urging I would have never gone onstage that night. My invisible friend MADE ME do it! Thanks buddy!

I've done just under three thousand stand-up shows since. These days my imaginary friends are less insistent. They still talk to me and suggest jokes on various subjects. And, except for when my latest imaginary friend absolutely insisted I write down these remembrances, I really don't feel compelled to comply, but once again, He made me do it! The moral to my story is: People who can't believe in imaginary friends equal BAD! And folks who can believe equal GOOD! End Story!

(This tale is dedicated to our imaginary friends, everywhere)

Lesson fifteen: Use your second best joke to open. You need to always open with a predictable laugh. This is always the top priority, so don't risk an adlib as your opening effort. Once you've opened your show well, then you can re-create the stimulus that made you want to respond, and throw in your adlib. (You've worked long and hard to get jokes you can depend on. Do you really want to try the first thing that comes into your silly head tonight?)

How to Get Happy!

Hi, I'm Endorphin Man! (tant-da-tadaa) I've invited you here to make you happy! Thanks for coming. Today's lesson is: "How to **make yourself** happy, in four easy Steps." If you buy the premise, you buy the bit. Don't you want to be happy?

You remember what happy is, don'tcha? Happy is that feeling you get when you finally find the TV remote or realize your phone bill's already paid. Happy is that fuzzy feeling inside, like when your cats purr, or you have a Saturday night date. Happy is when you realize the cops are pulling over the guy behind you. Now, you get it. Happy is when you realize that in the vast struggle between them and you…you won this one! Hooray! Happy is a game, and you're ahead, one to nothing.

The only preparation we need is some reasonable calm about you. This technique is called positive visualization. I'm going to ask you to remember certain times in your life, in a certain order. All those cool, natural endorphins, serotonins, and dopey-minis in your brain will start rushing around, cruising to get you in a better mood. They don't know you aren't happy. They live for this! Ready to be happy?

Make your face calm. Take a breath. Without moving your face, think of smiling. Take a breath. Without moving your face, smile a little. Take a breath. Now, smile using just the lower half of your face. Take a breath. Now, smile using all your face. If someone tells you this is meditation, they are confused. Ask them to check their taxes, go away, you're busy. Take a breath. Was that hard? I don't think so. But, it was step one. (Tant-da-tadaa) Remember step one: calm, take a breath, and *smile*.

Step two requires you to re-create how Disney kept Tinkerbell alive. Take a deep breath. Remember all the kids saying: "I believe!" Remember? And Tinkerbell's light got brighter and brighter. Smile. It's the same here. Do you believe you can make yourself happy? Smile. If you want to be happy, say: "I believe!" Don't forget step two: It's you, who must believe you can make yourself happy**.** Smile again.

Step three requires you to remember the last time you had a pocket full of money. Take a breath. If you can't remember anything like this, pretend you're Oprah! Smile. You could buy anything you want. Remember. Take a breath. Smile. Remember step three: If you don't have money now, pretend you're Oprah**.** Smile.

Step four requires you to remember the last time you had great, ultra-fine sex. No, not that one. Nope, not that time, either. You had tights on! Yep! That one! Yep! That one. Or, that one, Flight 26 out of Denver. Yes. Pick one of those. Take a breath. Smile. Remember? That was kooky! Smile. Take a breath. Smile. At this very moment, your brain chemicals are swooshing to various receptor points, just begging to plug in. Take a breath. Smile. Remember. Relax, we're half way home.

It's called sense memory. If someone says this is auto-erotica, tell them to stop spying on you. Ask them to do your laundry, go away, you're busy. Remember step four: Remember fondly, one event. Remember. Take a breath. Smile. If you've had some good times, you can always program yourself for more.

Summarizing: when you want to get happy, do these things, deliberately. Smile. Take a breath. Say: "I believe!" Smile. Take a breath. Pretend that you are Oprah. Smile. Take a breath. Remember when you had your legs way up there? Smile. Take a breath. Don't you feel happier now? I sure do. Dial that depression back a bit! It's really up to you. You've got a happy factory in your head. Use it.

This has been your pal, Endorphin Man. (Tant-da-tadaa) now you know the secret. If someone tells you this is yoga, hypnosis, or voodoo, I admit they're partially right. But, they're just jealous. They can't possibly be as happy as us. So, teach them our trick. Understand, you can choose! Happiness exists only in that weird eight inches of real estate that you call your head. It's your head. Keep it clean and keep it happy. I'll see you next time, same neural channel. (Tant-da-tadaa) Get Happy!

Lesson sixteen: Judaism teaches me: there is but one God. Buddhism teaches me: all humans are suffering. Islam teaches me: to be compassionate. Shinto teaches me: to venerate my ancestors and elders. Christianity teaches me: to love my brothers and sisters. Stand-up comedy has taught me: We are all the same when we laugh.

Grandpa's Promise

(Finding answers to why he never came home)

(10,000 miles from his home I wept, and saluted his grave. Even though I never knew him, I've always struggled with the hole he left in my mother's life. Now, on this windy bluff, overlooking Manila Bay, I wanted some answers from Major Van Frederick Houston. So, I decided to ask him.)

On a whirlwind tour of 12 countries and some 43 bases, I felt proud to do some comedy shows for our American troops so far from home. Our tour went so fast. I toured every federal post on the west coast my security clearance allowed. After whizzing through Korea and Japan, we went to the Philippines. How cool! My family history intersects the Pacific nations for four generations, so this was a heaven-sent chance. My Dad was there during Viet Nam, and Mom's dad was an Army Major who became a prisoner of war in WWII. (My nephew would serve there too!) Now, I was visiting. Great! I had some questions.

With two days off before my next show, I decided to search cemeteries for a clue about my mother's father. I inquired and received a recommendation for an independent cabbie named Frado. He knew 3 of the 5 cemeteries I wanted to visit, so off we went. After no results at the first three, Frado asked me why I was doing this. I told him: My grandfather was captured and held as a POW on Luzon in 1942. My Mom had only two letters before he was reported killed. I was here to find out why he never came home to her. Frado said that his grandfather too, had been killed fighting in the same area. He then said he'd heard of one more place to search. So we went to The *Cemetery of Heroes*, marked by some big, rolling hills, looking southwest at the gusty Bataan peninsula. The Sergeant of the Guard politely checked my ID and clearance credentials, and showed me where to look. After fluttering my way through several large box files, I finally found a card that read: Houston, Van Frederick U.S. Army Major Infantry- Texas ASN #0188982 Awarded Purple Heart, Killed in Action Oct. 24, 1944, Pillar 8, Section 52, and Plot #1

The Officer of The Day arranged an escort to the indicated area and specific marker.

Overlooking Manila Bay, hundreds of feet above roaring waves, stands an incredibly beautiful, white marble and brass pillar monument to fallen American soldiers. Grandfather was listed in the first column of Texans who gave their best and last. The escorts gave me room to pray, and I did. I told the Major that my Mom loved him and missed him. I thanked my grandfather for his service to America. I asked Van if he would answer some questions for his grandson. He said: "OK!" I asked him, what happened to you? You survived the Bataan Death March! You survived that horrible POW camp! (O'Donnell) I asked why he didn't come home to his daughter. I asked Van: "Why did you do all of this?"

Well, I guess as a Major in the Infantry of the United States army, he had become a man of few words. All I can remember he told me was: **"I did what I had to do! I followed my orders, I did my duty!"** My questions that could be answered were answered. Having the wonderful society to live in that I do, I finally understood. Yes, Major Van Houston and many thousands like him did their duty. They made the world safe for all of us. From Mecca to Manila, from Jerusalem to Rusk, Texas, we are all safer for what they did. It's so difficult to repay them. It's hard to say why little girls and boys have to grow up without their fathers. I promised Van I would tell his wife and only daughter exactly where he was. I again, promised to tell them that he had done his duty. I took some pictures to bring to Mom and Mom's Mom. Then, I had to leave him there, like many Americans who left loved ones on distant shores. I keep my promise to Grandpa still, and I will tell anyone who'll listen about those who did their duty, who never came home. I wept and saluted this man who I never knew. I will always remember this! Thank you Major Houston! Thank you to all of you who never came home to your daughters. Then, my friend Frado and I went to visit his grandfather's nearby grave. We just wanted to say thanks to him too.

Lesson seventeen: Take as many gigs as you can get. Once in a while, a gig may teach you something you need to know; that you don't know even know you need to know. Know what I mean? Turns out, if I hadn't been telling jokes overseas, none of this would have ever happened for my family.

Searching for Some Laughs!

(A biased book review)

Title: **"I'm dying Up Here!"**

Author: William Knodelseder

Published by: Pereus Book Group

Public Affairs Books.com

Jacket Design by Pete Garceau

Available online, and as an E-book.

In 1979, a handful of L.A. standup comics, who I still refer to as the Fabulous Fourteen, tried to blackmail a comedy club owner into paying cash for their services. It was a quasi-labor dispute argued by huge egos on both sides. "I'm Dying up Here!" is a story about comics' dreams realized, and some of those more firmly clutched dreams, frustrated.

Virtually all L.A comics went on "Comedy Strike." "NO BUCKS…NO YUCKS!" was their battle cry! Nine comics, of whom I was one, stayed with The World Famous Comedy Store. History has taught me this situation was akin to a bunch of Neanderthals taking ten seconds to assemble a nitroglycerin bomb. Inevitable mayhem and consequences ensued. Those blackmailing comics failed, and from the 12th floor of the Hyatt Hotel next door, a lowly wannabe (on strike) jumped to his lonely death.

It's my opinion that one of the Fabulous Fourteen, with whom I played on that same club's celebrity basketball team, is responsible in part, for that neurotic comic's sad and violent death. It's simply my opinion, but I was there! Read this incredible book to form your own opinion.

The unpredictable and roiling surf of publicity for "I'm Dying up Here!" has washed me out of retirement. Today, I choose to stand with The Comedy Store, as I always have. I always will. The author has interviewed me, and mentions me in his book several times. Respecting the art of full disclosure, I admit that I like Bill Knodelseder, and that I admire Bill Knodelseder! Bill the K sent me a thank you note for attending his book-signing event with my beautiful internet radio producer. This is my reply to him:

Hi Bill! (I loved the shoes you wore!)

I had an unbelievable blast at the Book Soup signing event. Who expected that kinda crowd and that many sales? Besides you, turns out I knew seven people there. Of all comics to be there, I had, in my caveman days, wanted to sleep w/ Susan Sweezter and Rachel, and now they probably both out earn me! C'est la vie! Brad Sanders and I had a talk that had waited 30 years. Same result as last time. I support The Comedy Store, and he doesn't! But I still like him. No grudges felt here. Argus Hamilton barely recognized me, and was shocked I was *following* him later, in the Original Room of The Comedy Store.

Also at Book Soup, standing in the back, by the register, was the owner of L.A.'s very popular Laff Factory, Jaime. He was very cordial, and invited me to call in for spots.

Bill, in your talk, promoting your book, you got nine good laughs…Nice shootin', Tex!

When I get my swing back, maybe you'll go to a show with me. Bill, I'd love to make you laugh. Since you are the most informed (about standup) media-ist I know, and one of the smartest guys I know, *and* I'm still hoping to get some coaching on my writing from you, here's some of that weirdo back-story to our shared Tuesday night:

Two days before, I showed up 2 hours early for Amateur Night Sunday at The Comedy Store Sunset. I used an unknown part of my name, and after 2 1/2 hours, *failed* to get a spot. The next day, I called in my availabilities to Tommy, Mitzi's comic coordinator. (Mitzi Shore, Pauly's mom, is the sole owner and operator of The Comedy Store on Sunset Blvd.) He growled at me: "We don't use veteran comics here, we grow our own!" Not expressing much hope, Tommy said he would talk to Mitzi, but that I shouldn't be hopeful. I waited. Usually, the comics call in after 10 am Tuesday to see if they got any spots. I waited. Surprisingly, Tommy himself called me back around 11 PM Monday night saying that when he told Mitzi about my request for stage time, she gave a loud: "Oh, My Godddd!" (Insert your best Mitzi voice here!) Good Lord in Heaven, she still remembers Lue!

My appearance following Argus was the result. It was Mitzi's way of welcoming me back, and making me feel comfortable to let the venerable Argie bring me on stage. (I had coached him on several of his Tonight Show performances.) Tommy said to park in our lot and take Mitzi's spot. This is a very rare honor for an old MC and doorman. A nice kid named Matt stopped me at the parking lot entrance, and said: "Are you Mr. Deck?" Another nice kid named Adam at the cover booth said: "You must be Lue! Come on in! You're on at 9:30." The effervescent piano player named Steve smiled and said, "Welcome back to The Original!" This was an amazing greeting from strangers who were doing the exact same job I had thirty years ago. Obviously, my way had been prepared! God Bless you Mitzi! Thanks, Tommy!

As I told you for your book, Argus Hamilton was my big brother at The Comedy Store in the '70's and '80's. As paid regulars, with assigned set times, we showed up ready to do our jobs after your book signing. It was very early, his opener sucked, and he didn't stay because he leaves right after his set, according to his habits. But even after thirty years, Argus made me laugh three or four times. And, for a crowd of about 40 thirty somethings, I did pretty well, Thank God!

On Wednesday, the owner of The Laff Factory, Jaime Mizeada left me a message with very warm instructions. On Thursday, The Laff Factory took my avails. Friday, I got an email from my online editor asking me if I'd like to start submitting some stories again. The Laff Factory's comic coordinator, a lovely Cecily said she'd call back with gigs next week or so. And I had sex twice this week! Will the miracles ever stop? Somehow I knew there would be waves about "I'm dying up here!" and I definitely planned to surf them.

It seems (Xxx Xxxx) (the part of my real name I used for Amateur Night) has no standing in L.A. standup, circles but evidently, the real Lue Deck does. I knew this vital fact in my heart of hearts. But, since I'd gotten hurt, I was afraid to do anything about it. At first, it was such an honor when you interviewed me. Later, it was a smokin' reminder to me about what I've accomplished in standup, and who I really was inside, and what I'd done lately, that I began to think you gave me an Intellectual hot foot! Well, thank you Bill! I'm certainly hopping around a lot now.

Your book has helped the way I feel about the strike, my act, my career, and my life. You sly writer guys are tricky. Bill, you made me remember, feel, and think, and get off my butt! Wow, Buddy, Thanks!

For the record, evidently I *was* home grown at The Comedy Store, but if I hadn't met and talked to you so much, I would not have gone back! It was you, not your book! Call me anytime! Your pal in Red Shoes, Lue (recently out of retirement)

To me, a new kid, the whole strike thing was stupid. In college, I found out what a labor union is, and how you form one. That mob-rule shouting bunch was not a labor movement. It still isn't, and it never will be. Comics need to learn to negotiate for themselves, or get an agent who can. If you are really a big shot in stand-up, then damn it - Stand tall! You should act like one.

Looking back to that crazy mix-up, I know all of the Fabulous Fourteen actually deserved to be paid for doing their acts at The Comedy Store. They were the funniest people in the world! Another twenty or so unknown names deserved it too. I'm convinced their mistake was in calling on the whole Los Angeles comic population to sacrifice themselves for individuals who were actually making it already. Drawing in loads of undeserving and not-ready-yet acts (like me!) into a miscalculated and pseudo-labor Ponzi scheme certainly doomed all of their legitimate grievances. But then, the decade of disco was looming on us all, and the most insecure ones amongst us just panicked!

If you ever see me doing a show, ask me afterwards about the time during the strike when many of my pals and fellow acts were trying to get me to do a honorary and ceremonial circuit around the picket line holding one of their signs. I had just taken a smoke break in front of The Main Room, following a whole hour onstage with Mitzi's new idea: group comedy. (You see, around the Store, we never, ever use the term: Improv. Never! Ever!) As I surveyed a group of mostly my peers, a friendly face saw a chance to be both political and funny at the same time. Thom Sharp, from Detroit, hoped to convert to the striker's side, the youngest and least seasoned act of the entire doorman staff: "Mitzi's boys!" And I will love him until the day I die for what he did. Thom Sharp started to, and got most of the picketers to start chanting their new labor slogan: Free Lue Deck! Free Lue Deck! Free Lue Deck! Sure, I walked the picket line for almost two complete loops! Hey, I'm Polish! Just to show solidarity. Mitzi caught me, and then I ran inside to do my late Belly Room set, like a freshman. But I still remember, and I loved it!

The Fabulous Fourteen were played by: Jay Leno, David Letterman, Elayne Boozler, Gallagher, Marsha Warfield, Paul Mooney, Tim Reid, Johnny Dark, Johnny Witherspoon, Brad Sanders, Thom Sharp, Richard Lewis, George Miller, and lastly Tom Dreesen.

The Nine comics who stayed with Mitzi were played by: Argus Hamilton, Mike Binder, Ollie Joe Prater, Harris Peet, Mitchell Walters, Yakov Smirnoff, Biff Maynard, Alan Stephans, and me, Lue Deck. I salute these nine St. Crispin's Day warriors. We few!

It is my heartfelt recommendation that comedy fans should read "I'm dying up here!" But, don't mind me; I'm just searching for some laughs in L.A. See you all at The Comedy Store. I'll be the one in Red Shoes. And, ironically, I am not dying up here!

Lesson eighteen: Develop TV jokes and nightclub jokes. Your first jobs will be in clubs, so when you need to, be prepared to get earthy for drinking crowds. Organize your jokes into similar topic sections called bits, then your bits into five minute hunks, then your hunks into fifteen minute sets. And so on.

I'm Still Standing!

When last I left you, I was holding a handful of miracles. In the ensuing week, I realized it just couldn't last. I was right. To quickly review, here's some of the crazy miracles to give you some perspective:

I was hurt real bad, but now, I'm getting better and stronger. My job was traveling the planet making people laugh. Now, I want my job back. A renowned author published a book about the Great Comedy Strike and interviewed me. I asked to go on at The Laugh Factory, and the gentlemanly Jaime, the owner, said yes! I got my Internet column back at TheCheers.org.I asked to go on at The Comedy Store in L.A. and they let me. (And gave me parking!) I asked to go on again, and the great and powerful Tommy said yes. (And Matt the God of Parking welcomed me warmly, which was another miracle.)

And then the miracles stopped. Surprise! As I said, Standup is a harsh mistress.

The evening caromed past me like a Quentin Tarantino flick, eight seconds pathetic alternating with eight funny seconds…for four and half-hours! It felt like a dream that wouldn't end, you know…like a Quentin Tarantino flick. I remembered that I had promised not to do any Pauly Shore jokes. Good Christ, who do I think I am? An early arrival At the World Famous Comedy Store gave me an eagle eye view for the greatest zoo show in the world. We've got the most incredible casting pool in the known universe in L.A. Dreamers, droolers, drinkers, stoners, Rappers, schitzos, those that are wannabe(s) and those lucky few who are soon to be(s) …you can see an incredible array of acts here. Sunday & Mondays are Open Mike in the Original Room until 10 PM. But, The Main Room and The Belly Room feature specialty shows. A veritable multiplex of standup acts. Who do I think I am?

After a couple hours, the amateur show gives way to guest spots and paid regulars. I was pleasantly surprised to count about forty hearty souls hanging in to catch the owner's choice part of the show. (What we used to call "Mitzi's boys") I told myself to get ready. I remembered that I had promised not to do any Pauly Shore jokes. Good Christ, who do I think I am?

Catching a break, it turns out that I knew the Master of Ceremonies from long, long ago. A snappy dresser then, and now, it was the well-known and beloved Frazier Smith. He was funny on the FM then, and now he's learned to be funny onstage. Another miracle. Most Radio Boys don't make it as stand-ups, but Frazier is the exception. I was glad to see him.

After exchanging greetings (and checking each other for telltale plastic surgery wounds) Mr. Smith told me I would go on after the Vegas act and guest performer. I gave him a card with my credits for my introduction. He looked at me like I was from El Salvador. You see, The Comedy Store is like an artist's colony. But, it's an artist's colony that eats its own slower members of the herd. I reminded myself to stay focused and not get eaten.

I try to keep an eye on the preceding acts so I won't repeat a premise, but after a while, I just couldn't watch anymore. The Vegas act bummed the room out, then made 'em happy and left the stage. The MC says he's been ordered to put one of the staff on next…Sorry! A funny Asian kid went on, smoothed through seven minutes. He got good laughs. The MC brought on another staff comic and he got good laughs too. And another, and another. Sorry! Now, its 11 PM…I got here at 9 PM, and my 10 PM set will be after 11:30. Fasten your seat belts everybody, this is going to be a bumpy ride! The crowd had grown to about fifty. I just kept moving, as I was still hoping not to get eaten.

I walked the entire Comedy Store complex repeating my material to myself, while checking my key word list for this set. I crossed paths with ten other comics doing the same thing. During the show, backstage in The Main Room, I greeted the ghost there. He remembered me, which was sweet after all these years, and he promised not to scare me too much that night. Now I owe him a damn favor.

The upstairs Belly Room was totally empty. I had helped turn this storeroom into a great stage featuring countless great comediennes. I had also been allowed to learn my craft on this stage, and I cannot wait until I get a show in there again. Come by the Belly Room sometime. You won't be disappointed. Happily, I hurried back to the Original Room where I got my start.

Frazier the MC, finally told me one more act, and then I'd be next. Then, I got eaten. The guest performer was Bobby Lee of MAD-TV fame. As he began his set, another twenty young ladies jammed the room to watch him. I hadn't seen girls on the hunt like that since Brad Pitt did those skimpy underwear ads. On TV and live, Bobby Lee is one courageous comic, and he did twenty minutes or so. Bobby Lee, who reminds me of an equally courageous Andy Kaufman, murdered the room. Like me, Bobby is a former doorman for the Comedy Store, so I was proud of him. But he murdered the room. Holy Crap! The massive audience, now sated by Bobby, split the room like somebody had cut a big one. Qui coupe le fromage? Now it was 12:28 AM, and I being introduced. Oh God, help me…I'm an early act. The audacity! Who do I think I am?

Evidently, our esteemed MC, Mr. Frazier Smith knew who I was. This experienced performer not only quieted the entire room, (which had shrunk to only eight people) but then, he gave me a warm, slow, respectful introduction. (Missing the facts by a mile.) Because Frazier had taken his time, many of the doormen and other paid acts flooded the back of the room to support me. Even Argus. The audience (all eight of them) re-focused and were nice. I opened my act in Spanish and ironically the crowd looked at me like I was from El Salvador. My three best punch lines in Spanish got nice laughs! *"Yo soy El Gringo con corazon! You soy muy guappo! Frazier Smith es Chupacabra! Ayudame! Ayudame!"* I told the crowd that the MC told me it was "Spanish Only" night. A decent laugh. Then I moved on to my real language which is English, I think. Everybody say **"Hi LUE!"**

"Hi folks! My name's Lue. To me, being a gentleman means avoiding the use of profanity and cuss words………. Until I absolutely, (bleeping) have to! No S**t!"

I didn't want to use the f and s bombs, but right at that moment (12:32 AM) I felt like I needed some of that street cred. (Whatever that is.) I did the quick stuff from my act that I thought I could count on. Most of those paying attention laughed for me. I brought the room back. My time flew past.

Everybody say **"Bye LUE!"** then I was offstage. Not great…not bad. The next act did not respond when introduced, and then suddenly POOF! I was gone and forgotten. On to the next act. But, I didn't get eaten in a situation that I should have been. For the millionth time in my zany career, I got lucky. I got lucky, and live to be funny another day. One more miracle. Thank you Lord.

That's two shows. It's only two. But, I hadn't done any shows in twenty-four months. The adrenaline residue took hours to wear off, and I didn't get to sleep until 5 AM. I await news of my scheduled times from the Laugh Factory. I've listened to the tape of my last show six times, just to take out jokes that didn't work. Do you think this is easy? Do I look fat in these clothes? I just want to do better shows. I'm jumpy and nervous. I wish I had nicer red shoes. Do I need a haircut? Such is the funny life in Hollywood.

I'm not really in show business. I just live in L.A for the **frustration!**

It's like I told you earlier: Standup comedy is a harsh mistress. But she does kiss well. And amazingly enough, I'm still standing!

Lesson nineteen: Middle acts should start quickly and finish faster. No matter how well you're doing, cut two minutes, and finish early! Close with your best bit, exit, and then tell the headliner that the crowd will love him. Thank the club owner or booker, or both, for the job, then watch the closing act, and analyze his technique.

The Queen of Comedy!

(Inventor of the Funniest Place on Earth!)

When any of three, four, or five generations of stand-up comics sit on the ground telling tall tales of the sad death of comedy clubs, Mitzi Shore's name inevitably comes up. How could it not?

The David Lettermans, Robin Williamses, the Richard Pryors, the Gary Shandlings, the Roseanne Barrs, and other wannabe hopefuls (like me!) all have a few wild stories to re-tell about the Queen of Comedy, founder of Hollywood's World Famous Comedy Store.

The stand-up comedian factory on Sunset Blvd. was born in the early 70's when Mitzi started working her unique magic. It continues today, nightly, hilariously, and God and Mitzi willing, eternally! When you hear of luminaries like the famous movie producer: David O. Selznik, or the vaudeville and burlesque impresario: Flo Ziegfeld, we may want to include and add some laurels for Mitzi Shore. Show biz history should note that Mitzi touched and aided as many, if not more, laughter- filled comedian's careers. A lot of Americans remember some of their educational moments fondly. For me, and countless other comics, Mitzi, and The Comedy Store (that she so expertly molded and nurtured) was the best teacher and school I ever had.

Mitzi's list of innovations is prodigious! (Continuous comedy all night. Her simple stage layout: black curtain, single mic, solo pianist. {Brick walls are so cheap!} Cable TV specials. Her come-back shows featuring stand-up greats: Mort Sahl, Soupy Sales, David Frye, Dick Gregory, and Rodney Dangerfield. Network development deals for emerging acts. The Belly Room, to encourage more lady stand-ups. Michael Keaton as Batman, Paul Mooney, George Miller, Jimmy Walker, Ben Bailey of Cash Cab fame, Jim Carrey, and Andy "Dice" Clay.

Go to the Comedy Store website, or better yet, go to the actual Funniest Place on Earth at 8433 Sunset Blvd. in Los Angeles. You might even see the Pauly Shore perform! Our three separate showrooms offer the possibility to watch the next Steve Harvey, Jeff Foxworthy, or Ellen DeGeneres strut their stuff. The Original Room show offers more than 15 acts each night. The Belly Room upstairs used to be exclusively for female comics, (like Whoopi Goldberg and Lois Bromfield) but has evolved to present them, and the cutting edge in New Age stand-ups. The Main Room used to be the legendary "Ciro's" in the 1930's and 40's. Our storied alumni include Sinatra, Dean Martin and Jerry Lewis, Victor Borge, Buddy Rich and his orchestra, Richard Pryor (at his best), Chevy Chase, Johnny Witherspoon, Tim Reid, Sam Kinnison, Bobby Lee, Jay Leno, and many more incredible names than even Sammy Shore could shake a stick at!

If you've ever wondered where all those funny people come from, the answer is everywhere! But, for a stand-up to get anywhere in Hollywood, it takes a workable path. It takes a trail, a road. And, in this particular case, all should know that the super highway autobahn named The Comedy Store was designed and built by the Queen of Comedy: Mitzi Shore! Somebody should say thanks to her! Any of her comics who have a memory or a conscious really should respond.

With poor health, Mitzi is seldom seen in her funny domain in the last couple of years. But, most experienced eyes can still spot her expert hand on the tiller and helm. (Tiller and Helm, wasn't that the names that The Smothers Brothers used when they started?) How about an asterisk or footnote for the dominance of her Comedy Store franchises in the 70's, 80's, 90's, and oughties? How about a getting a star on the Hollywood Walk of Fame for the Comedy Store's Mitzi Shore? How about it? It's the next logical step. Soon!

Hoards of working comics owe their comedic control and self-marketing skills to The Comedy Store system. I do! (All 2,977 paid shows in 45 states and 23 countries in which I was privileged to perform.) At this point, the very least her graduates and alumni can do, is to acknowledge Mitzi's importance in their lives and careers. Just call her, write her, or email her! Or just say "Hi" to her during their talk show gigs, and wish her, and The Comedy Store, well. We really all owe this little thing to her, don't we? I want to nominate her for a star on The Walk of Fame!

Thanks Mitzi! We love you! Get well soon!

Lue Deck (an original Mitzi Shore production)

The Comic in Red Shoes

Home Club: Comedy Store Sunset. 1975-2014

Lesson twenty: Since a stand-up can only get better by performing, you should figure out how to get as many shows, as quickly as you can! Having a home club is unbelievably helpful! Find a place where they like you!

CSPAN Called Me!

CSPAN, the venerable watch keepers of America's Congress, is celebrating the twenty-fifth anniversary of its flagship cable TV show: Washington Journal, on Friday, Oct. 7th with a 25-hour marathon extravaganza. Since its inception in 1980, over a half million callers have participated, and last week, They called ME!

To emphasize the "call-in" segments of the show, the powers-that-be at Washington Journal decided to have an essay contest with the theme: "Why I watch and participate!" I entered, using Snail Mail, rather than E-mail, because my screen name has Laffs in it, and just this one time, (besides at the bank.) I actually wanted to be taken seriously.

The contest rules stipulated a 250-word essay, which yielded 25 winners, and one grand prizewinner. The grand prizewinner is invited, with all expenses paid, to our nation's capital to co-host a segment of Washington Journal. The other lucky 25 winners will be interviewed, one per hour, on air, and will each get to read their precious essay to the whole wide world. Wow!

Last week, some 26 days after I mailed my entry, the phone rang. CSPAN's Director of Media, a kind and helpful Ms. Jennifer Moire called to inform me that I was one of the additional 25 winners. Wow! She answered my questions and told me when to expect a call for my interview with one of the Washington Journal's regular hosts. Be still my heart, is it Brian Lamb?

This week, one of the kindest, most sincere, and most gracious ladies of our time, Ms. Susan Swain called with a gleam in her voice. At least it seemed that way to me. She took her time with me, knowing in the goodness of her heart, all the contest winners would be thrilled to, at last, be an acknowledged partner with so esteemed a media team. Susan, as she said I could address her, briefed me as to how the interview would progress, and She even offered me an opportunity to re-do my reading, if necessary. I told her: I am Lue Deck, The Comic in Red Shoes, and I was very prepared.

I asked Susan if I, jokingly, could propose that somebody, anybody, would nominate the founder of CSPAN, Mr. Brian Lamb, for The Presidential Medal of Freedom. Well, Brian must run a very tight ship over a CSPAN, because Susan reacted like I had just shot her dog. "No, no, no, Brian never wants to be in the spotlight!" Well, three no's in a row convinced me this was a dead-end path, so I raise the idea here. Write your Congressman!

I read my essay and even managed to get a national plug in for The Cheers.org as well. Any of my devoted readers will spot some of my article titles within my essay. It's like Where's Waldo…with red shoes. Off the air, I managed to make Susan laugh with a couple of selected jokes I thought she'd go for. "Did you hear they're actually going to make Rocky 6? Yeah, in Rocky 6, this time, Rocky fights osteoporosis!" Susan laughed. "The price of gasoline is so high in America now…We're gonna have to invade three more countries!" Susan gasped a little, but she did laugh!

My essay wasn't intended to be funny. It was intended to honor CSPAN. If you ever listen to Washington Journal, you'll soon realize that some of the smartest people in the world call in, and so do some of the most narrow-minded people. Regular viewers get used to discerning which is which. I'm the smart ass one. My interview will air on Friday, October 7th at 11pm PDT Wow! Won't you join us? Feel free to call in. My genuine thanks to the lovely Jennifer Moire, the talented Susan Swain, and the reclusive Brian Lamb over at CSPAN.

A copy of my essay (with the jokes I edited out for CSPAN, now appearing only here, in italics) is included at the end of this article.

Mute your TV, please!

Washington Journal contributes to an informed electorate. People get to see our democratic republic evolve its own laws. It's remarkably like watching our original Constitutional Convention, in person. *(Except that Washington Journal's hosts also act as wrestling referees)*

If our Founding Fathers were alive today, they would all be watching, muttering, and calling into Washington Journal! *(Can't you just see Brian trying to enforce the "30 days between calls" rule on Thomas Jefferson or Aaron Burr?)*

Uniquely, this program acts as a social stethoscope, providing everyone, every day, an opportunity to hear the American heartbeat! *(The heartbeat with high cholesterol and inflated blood pressure)*

Observing our diverse newspapers, WJ'saudience gets to ponder what's happening, all over our country, warts and all. The Hotline and Roll Call segments play like crazy sports bloopers. More please! Heroically, the only chance some of our citizens will ever get to speak out in public, for what they believe, is on WJ! Never lose that, please!

As long as one remembers to MUTE one's TV, anyone can join in! *(Which one in four usually forgets to do, those morons!)*

Some callers parrot their party line; others want answers. WJ remains impartial, using separate lines for opposing viewpoints, with one extra line for those oh, so wacky others. These far-flung seekers turn out to be the ultimate support groups. By each show's end, all sides receive almost equal time. It's fair. WJ gets loud, it's often rowdy, but it's chock full of info and C-Span's hosts are always fair. *(The oh, so wacky others can include: Misfits, Mavericks, ETs, hobos, Libertarians, and former Gov. Jessie Ventura, but not Pat Buchanan!)*

This is why I watch and participate. I watched Washington Journal on its first day, I watched it yesterday, and if America isOK, I'll watch Washington Journal tomorrow. *(Ok, maybe I'm just a little obsessed!)*

Wow, it really happened, CSPAN actually called little ole ME!

Lesson twenty-one: Waiting for the right moment is the second most important thing a comic can do. (The first is focusing on telling your jokes correctly.) Not everybody has great timing, but good timing can be learned and improved. Recognizing **when** *to speak, or do, is practiced best by arriving at the club early, by being ready to answer your introduction, and getting to the microphone on time.*

RENT MY BODY?

(Shut up, Monkey Brain!)

As he put his red van in park and turned off the engine, Willy realized that someone had just rented his body…again! Damn, he always felt so cheap afterwards. He had accepted all the loony baggage that came with it when he finally signed the trust papers, but even after dozens of rentals, the aftershock effects still left him feeling whorish and white trashy. But, in the next moment, Willy was curious about how it had gone for his customer. Did the political jokes work? Were there hecklers?

Willy struggled to find his cane. Such was life in Hobble land. Willy flashed on his father, a real old school engineer type. He could still hear Dad urging him: "Life is tough! Get used to it! Rub some dirt on it! Now, walk it off!" Willy smiled and thought for the millionth time: "Good advice." Monkey brain says: "…no matter how annoying it happened to be…every time!" He dragged himself out and smiled at the Aerostar again.

Ole Red had carried him safely from Savannah to Spokane, from Toledo to Tijuana, from the UP to the OC! Such was life for a working standup comic. Hundreds of cities, thousands of shows, this old hoss never failed him on the comedy trail. Willy mused about all the jokes he'd written while driving Red to his next gig. "Yeah, those Texas jokes!" Again, he tried to judge how his jokes and act had played for the rentee. He turned and worked his way up painfully to his second floor loft.

ComedyFox.com had put up an old video of Willy's act in Louisville, Kentucky doing a killer set for The Nashville Network. Three things happened: 1) He got a great tape and a good paycheck 2) When it aired, his 5th cousins came out of the woodwork to borrow money (Really, I mean it, three big hairy "Deliverance" guys CAME OUT of the woodwork!) And 3) The CEO of RENT MY BODY emailed an offer of cash pay for play. Willy had never heard of digital memory replay. Evidently, some gadget guy in Silicon Valley figured out how to let people rent other people's best moments in life, and relive them, if properly digitally connected. Willy didn't really understand the process. Hey, he didn't even have a cell phone anymore. He didn't feel important enough. So, he had signed up. Anyhow, it paid most of the bills.

On the long way up an old, winding staircase, Willy was glad he'd had the van-wakeup clause inserted in his rental agreement. It was the tip-off that someone had rented his act. RENT MY BODY. What a concept! Wonder what Isaac Asimov would think about that. Willy again smiled, contemplating if his customer had a good time. He wondered if the nuclear proliferation joke worked. Boy, that particular joke needed a lot of sarcasm. Think Keith Olbermann on steroids. "Shut up monkey brain!"

Reaching the last 3 steps before his door, Willy groaned like a wounded wookie as he heard the loud snap that signaled his left knee was going on vacation, right now! It also meant he was going to fall…again. Damn it, he really hated getting old. Willy never saw the bleeping metal hand railing his forehead bounced off, but later he remembered what went through his mind. It was "…hope my cop jokes worked!"

When he came to, Willy's headache was the size of Memphis. Not the Memphis in Egypt, the one in Tennessee. (Some get confused.) He had been reliving a killer show in Louisville three years ago, before the car wreck. Onstage, stuff was going great. Folks liked his local references. Oh boy, there was a heckler! Willy liked hecklers because they were like a good steak dinner to him. If Willy made a heckler the butt of his show, the guy learned quick enough to shut up. (Hey Skippy, do I come down to Burger King, and bleep up your job?) Then, he turned stage left and saw his reflection in a bar mirror. He had red hair. And he was a woman. Wow, a woman had rented his act! "Oww!"

Willy's head felt like two reality stars banging skulls, arguing over more camera time. Why was he a girl in his dream? Because he had watched the video of that particular set so many times, Willy remembered seeing himself in the onstage mirror. And he was sure he wasn't a damn girl, now or then. "Owww!" His knees hurt as much as his poor punkin' head. It jumped through his short-circuited mind; could the red head be the one who just leased his act? His deal wasn't supposed to work like that, but what else could it be? Damn, she was good! Did she do the Viagra jokes?

Fumbling for keys and staggering through his front door. "Owww!" Willy knew he wouldn't have made it through the wreck surgeries without the dough from the rentals. But he hadn't expected all this. "What's happening to me?" This wasn't the first time Willy had felt this way. Since he'd grown so much as a teenager, four inches when he was fourteen, four inches when he was fifteen, Willy had been hitting his head on low-hanging stuff. Once, he stood up into a ceiling fan. He'd had so many skull injuries there was a dent in his head. He called it brain slosh when he couldn't remember. Like who he was, what he'd done, where he'd been. "I did what in a show, where, in 2003?" Maybe that's why the digital memory thingy worked so well for him. Willy had felt the panic of not knowing who you are, or where you are, for the first hour awake, more than he wanted to admit to himself, or anyone.

Willy checked his messages, mail, and email. Might as well have checked for bleeping messenger pigeons. Nothing. Monkey brain says: "Do something!" Shut up! Willy hated not performing. As a standup comic, Willy never met a gig he didn't like. Once any club or booking agent liked him, and/or his act, Willy would not say no to a show. To Willy, his standup act was the natural confluence of words and fun! To him, the only thing that mattered was getting his crowd laughing. That's how he measured his self-esteem for thirty years. He loved making up jokes when seeing new places, or meeting new folks. That's who he was. Any showroom, any stage! Willie hated giving that up. The holes it left in him felt like gunshots. After his body wore out, well, it was like an itch that couldn't be scratched, or a tickle in your damn throat that couldn't be coughed away, or a big gas bubble that was bound to embarrass you, or a…"Shut up, Monkey brain!" He slumped onto his favorite couch.

Willy was annoyed with himself. If he lets it get going, his damn monkey brain chatters at him nonstop. Here was a chance to avoid his good old buddy, or get down and party with Mr. Trouble. Sometimes, Willy and monkey brain would while away the endless hours on comedy tour by sarcastically testing new jokes or characters, on one another. Vastly amusing to them, not so much to those around. He had cultivated his monkey brain for years on tour to help him get juiced for the standup show each night. Now, it was Willy's worst time of the day for uninvited adrenaline, and then the inevitable depression at sunset. He accepted that he couldn't tour or do long shows anymore. Such was life after sixty. "Shut up!" But, most of the time Willy felt like he was just waiting around to die. What's the point? No raison d'être. (Whatever that means.) He joked that the first evening after he did die, what was left of his carcass would hump its way to the nearest comedy stage and do 30 minutes!

Then recently, his left knee, spine, two aortic veins, and head dent all thought they were a 1991 Buick, and just quit working! So, life is tough. Walk it off. Hold what you got. Make lemonade! "Shut up monkey brain!" Gradually, he settled back, and gratefully fell asleep without charting Leno and Letterman this time. As all identity flowed away, Willy smiled at himself and again puzzled Buddha's question: "What does one get when one plants rice?" The answer is obvious…rice. His simple insight is to understand that what you have in your life is exactly what you have previously planted. If you want something different in your life…plant the seeds for it, because you get and have exactly what you plant! (Monkey brain: Pretty sure the rice lesson is from an old episode of "Kung Fu")

So, if it happened that Willy woke up tomorrow and once again didn't know who he was, then he'd have to do his damndest to make sure that person was funny! Funny was all that counted to him. Even if Willy couldn't be funny anymore, someone else could. It was a weird bargain, but he could live with that. Semper funny! Willy called monkey brain a filthy name. "But, who was that red haired girl, anyway? Shut up monkey brain, please, just shut up!"

…blinking awake, He put his red van in park and turned off the engine. Willy quickly realized somebody had rented his body, again! Damn!

Lesson twenty-two: Learn to change your joke list like you were a NASCAR pit crew. The faster, the better. Interchangeability of jokes leads to interchangeability of your bits, and thereby your hunks too! Keep a dry erase board with your set list by your bed. Use it to keep your choices fresh in your mind.

I told Me Not to Do it!

(Would you change you?)

Old Lue sat by the desk, pondering the note. What should he say to himself? The last note didn't work as well as he'd hoped. He put his time travel gadget down on the bed for the umpteenth time and stared at it. He could only use it twice more to go back in time to help his younger self. And kid know-it-all hadn't listened much to the note on his first trip. Old Lue (at 45) wanted to find a way to convince young Lue (at 25) to avoid some of their/his worst mistakes on stand-up tour. Old Lue muttered "the young punk better pay attention this time or, I'll let him book that show in Haiti! That'll teach him!" After several frustrating hours, the room was a mess with partially discarded pizza boxes, cigarette butts, and pitifully crushed Pepsi cans strewn about. But, Lue had written five or six notes. Then, he balled them up and pitched them in/at/towards the trash can. Damn! What should he tell his younger self to avoid?

An alternately compulsed, (Yes, I know *compulsed* is not a word!) then driven Lue leaned past the mirror, and saw his reflection. Lue noticed that the jagged scar over his left eye was gone. He'd gotten that from a rowdy patron in Tupelo, Mississippi, who objected to a certain joke twenty years ago. It took 11 stitches, and the ER doctor had appeared at his next show. Later, she *did* him! So, he vividly remembered her, the ugly scar, and he remembered having the scar for years, and now the damn scar was gone. The scar was gone! Wow! Maybe the little snot did pay attention to the note. Lue thought: "If he told that Elvis joke in Tupelo, I knew he'd get beaten up. I did!" Cool! This might work.

Time travelers can't meet themselves in the past or future, or all hell starts breaking loose. So, Lue had worked out the note idea. Stand-up comics were always being given notes at their showrooms, clubs, and hotels. Notes to remind you about the birthday girl in the front row, or notes to meet someone at the bar, or notes to tell you to report to the manager, now! He looked at his time gadget again. After travelling back on Trip One, Lue paid a pretty hooker to pass his advice note to his younger self. (That did the trick, so to speak!) So, he knew he could get a bellman or doorman or barmaid to pass his improved note on Trip Two. He just needed to write a better note. Write a better note, moron! He was careful to use older bank notes for the tip, and get clothes that were just quirky enough to not be noticed. Not that Lue would admit to being obsessed, but he wanted to get things right this time, dammit!

The whole reason to pull this hair-brained stunt is now, at long last, Lue finally understood how stand-up comedy worked for him. When he looked back at his incredibly lucky life and lengthy career, he realized he had also wasted a humongous amount of struggle and time with some terrifically bad choices. Sure, those bad choices taught him how to adapt, improvise, and overcome dead-ends and problems, but he still wanted to save himself a buncha time and trouble. It's a Virgo thought, but these particular lessons were important, so he wanted his younger self to learn the moral to each, just a little quicker. So he/we/they could save some time. Being a working standup comic had given confidence, identity, and a damn fine livelihood. Lue wanted this to last forever. So he/we/they got better as a comic. Keep your eye on the damn prize! So, write a better note! Better!

Lue limped over and went through the trash can. He may wash his hands too much, but he was always willing to get his hands dirty sifting to find his best ideas. He wondered: if he was given a note and told not to do something…would he believe it? And would he do as he was advised? He just didn't know. I guess it's a "Buy the premise…buy the bit!" thingy. So, he didn't know if he'd do, or not do what the note said not to do. Gee, just thinking it through like that made his head hurt! Then, there was an unexpected knock at the door. Lue was puzzled for a second or two. It was the bellman with more pizza, Kools, and diet Pepsi. Lue tipped him a tenner. It was going to be a long night.

Starting the note was tricky. Lue had planned to use approaches that appealed to him when he was twenty-five. "Dear Lue: You can get funnier, faster by blah, blah!" "Dear Lue: You will double your bookings if blah, blah, and blah." Or "Dear Lue: If you want more sex, then blah, blah, blah!" He finally decided to use inside knowledge that only the two of them would know, understand and recognize. He would address the note to their/his long hidden middle name.

He completed the seventh list with the only item that all the previous lists had in common: **#1-Don't sleep with Mitzi!** (Mitzi Shore is the famous owner/impresario of L.A's Comedy Store, and having regular sex with her had killed numerous advancing careers.) **#2-Don't try to sleep with two casting directors at the same time!** (There goes your film career!) **#3-Endorphin Man is not real!** (It's a character, it's not a lifestyle!) **#4-Stay in YOUR hotel in Manila!** (There are times and places to have fun after the show. Luzon is neither!) **#5-Don't ever Rap in your act! Ever!** (No one who decides to rap in their standup act will be remembered, or ever re-hired!) **#6-In Show biz, be real nice to everyone on your way up!** (On your way down, you won't get the time.) Lastly, **#7-Don't marry that pretty cop from Tampa!** (Challenges are great, and lots of fun, but who's kidding whom here? Why show up for a damn pissing match, and find out that it's a gun fight?)

Lue looked at his seventh list. This ought to do it. This is the best advice he could devise for his younger self. Imagine the time, expense and grief that young Lue could avoid if he followed the advice on the new list. Trip Two should do the trick! He settled in to prepare his props. Note? Check! Cash? Check! Costume? Check! Time gadget? Check! Red Shoes? Check! Battle Plan? Check! Obsession? Check! OK, let's do this thing!

Ripping him from his OCD-like reverie, there was another knock at the door. Lue was instantly confused. No one knew he was here, except hotel staff. Suddenly, the right side of his head, just over his ear got real hot! That usually meant trouble for Lue. What's this? What did I do wrong now? He hid his time gadget and rushed over to the door. It was the bellman again, this time delivering a note, left at the front desk.

It was addressed to: Lue (at 45) Deck (He *says* he's a comedian!)

The Dunes Casino and Hotel- Room 3333 Las Vegas, NV. The note read:

"Hey Lue! This is the better note you were just thinking of! Buy the premise! Don't use the gadget now. Save Trip Two for later. The kid will figure it out. You did! I did! Let him make it. "We did!" You were a pretty good comic since him anyhoo! Thanks for working so damn hard! FYA: Here's your new bleeping list!"

#1-Leave the kid alone!

#2-When offered a gig, take it!

#3-Endorphin Man is real.

#4-Write your ass off.

#5-Forget the lady cop!

#6-Never do that Siegfried & Roy joke again!

#7-Use less boldface and go back on tour.

Hey look! The scar over your left eye is back!

Love yourself more,

Lue (at 65)

He looked and sure enough, the scar was back. He could take a hint. He'd leave the kid alone. Lue (at 45) packed up, but he was smiling. Maybe he could save some time some other way. Evidently, you could change **you**, if you were crazy enough. He checked out and headed for his next gig in Lexington, KY at the Two Keys Tavern.

Lesson twenty-three: To keep improving my act, I developed a technique called Spock's tri-corder. After three or four minutes on stage (having gotten some laughs) I would take the mic and step away from the crowd, tap my chest and say: "Ensign Lue Deck, reporting sir!"(While surreptitiously reading the crowd for interest, sympathetic faces, or distractions) If the read wasn't good, I'd draw attention to the problem. If my read was favorable, I'd say: "Yes Mr. Spock, it is time to read the crowd!" I'd let the crowd know I was reading them by pointing my imaginary tri-corder at them, then I'd say: "Pretty good Mr. Spock, but a few are confused." I'd nod and say: "Try what joke, Mr. Spock?" Then I'd laugh and say: "Mr. Spock, you're one funny bastard!" I'd continue my act until it was time to read the crowd again, every three or four minutes. I adjust my pace of delivery to keep the crowd focused on what I'm doing.

Things you should remember:

Stand-up format: MC/Opener-15 min. Feature act: 30 min. Headliner-45 min.

Learn to deal with hecklers. Keep a list of responses and come-backs!

Write and practice TV-G jokes, if you ever want to do TV.

Very few dirty stand-up acts get to Heaven.

Don't be surprised if the weasel in line in front of you is more successful.

Comedy teams prepare you to do single stand-up, because teams never last.

Slow learning stand-ups fall by the wayside. Pay attention!

If you aren't good at making opportunities for yourself, get someone who is.

Record your shows, and study them. It's the only way for you to get better.

Attitude acts usually have weak joke writing skills. Write better jokes.

When you get to a gig, it's on you to make a good outcome. Nobody else.

One third of all gigs are hell gigs. Get used to it! Find a way to be funny!

Dress nicely for your shows.

There are great jokes in everything that happens to you. Look for them!

Develop a duality to separate jokes from your real life.

Learn to make yourself happy. Sometimes you can use the same skill on your crowds.

Take every gig that is offered to you. What else is more important than improving?

If anyone remembers you, or your jokes, you've been blessed! What did you do?

As Bob Marley says: "Never give up the fight!"

Writing jokes leads to writing essays. Writing essays leads to writing books.

Did you plan for your future?

What would you change in your act? What would you change ten years from now?

What is your average LPM rate? Can you go faster?

Use a timer you can refer to during your show. Watch and adjust your pace if necessary!

Don't criticize your audience. Your criticism will make the crowd stop laughing for you.

If your crowd is still laughing, don't keep talking! Wait for it. (2-3-4!)

For demonstration and analysis, here are my jokes from a show in Louisville, KY. Watch my video on YouTube as you read. (Search for: Stand-up DECODED) In this 30 minute show, I averaged an LPM rate (Laughs per minute) of four to five! That's pretty fast, even for me, but it was a hot crowd. My tactical motivations behind each choice are in italics. There are nine jokes masquerading as adlibs. See if you can find them!

(I want to appear happy, energetic, and ready to go! I have my first joke primed and loaded. Watch, as I catch the wave of focus, aim, and fire. My idea is to take the momentum and prove I am worth this crowd's attention as quickly as I can. Many people form a first impression in the first five seconds, and half of the time, they do stick with it. I use that.)

Thanks for having me in Louisville. I love **Louisville!** My name is Lue, I wear red shoes, and I love this town. I love that thing you do for **pot smokers** at Christmas time, **Light up Louisville,** I really like that.

(I try not to risk an adlib as an opening joke, but the "light up" joke was a middle of the set adlib from a show six months before, that became a dependable local joke. It also matches the subject of my opener.)

I really love your town, but you really do have some messed up drivers here. I'm driving down, what do you call it? Bardstown Road… So, I stick my hand out the window to signal for a left turn, and this redhead takes the damn joint… **Right out of my hand!** Wow, keep it…**Officer!**

(My most dependable joke: "Outa my hand" and that's why I use it as an opener.)

Nice to be here, I'm from the South and I want to make some friends tonight. If you would: everybody say: "Hi Lue!" Yeah, let's rock this place!

(Using an opener that has the crowd respond in unison really builds focus fast.)

(I start with some biography jokes and the irony that shaped my humor.)

I'm from Atlanta, anybody ever hear of Atlanta? Atlanta is a strange town. Yeah, we had the Olympics, **only one bombing**!

To me, to live in Atlanta you have to fit one of two groups: either you're a yuppie or a redneck! Either your pickup truck has a satellite dish, or your Mercedes-Benz **has a gun rack!**

We used to have a law in Georgia determining what kind of sex you could have! Really, it was against the law to have sodomy or oral sex! And, if they caught you having it, they put you right in prison! Where you can get **all that stuff** you want! I think Bubba missed the damn point here!

(These jokes illustrates life's quirks and how I deal with them.)

Damn glad to be in Louisville this week, real happy, because I was in jail in Bowling Green **last week**. I had one of those awful days, I'm sure you've had 'em. I was driving up I-65, doing 95 in a 55 and **all of those numbers just bleeped me up!**

(I've cast myself as everyman to get the crowd to identify with my problems.)

I had a talk with the Kentucky State police. He was mad and yelling at me. "I want to see your driver's license, your registration, and your proof of insurance!" I must have gone through that glove box for 15 minutes, before I realized I was sitting in the front seat of **his** car! For a minute, I felt like Vanna White when no one gets a letter!

(These jokes are designed to show how I try to find the silver lining when confronted.)

Hey, guess what, I got free overnight accommodations, in the Bowling Green jail! Turns out, the next morning, I was **a minority**! Just me, in red shoes, and nine or 12 black guys. I was scared. I just stayed in the corner and kept quiet, until one of the biggest guys there, walked up and asked me: "What you in here for?" Again, I admit I was scared, I told him: "I've got AIDS… And **they've got no place to put me!**" He was so scared of me, after a couple minutes, I started chasing him around the cell!

(I try to get a joke from everywhere I visit, so the crowd gets the impression I perform all over.)

I've been traveling a lot, I got stopped at the Texas state border, seems like my car did not pass the inspection: **NO GUN-RACK!**

Got a ticket from a Texas state trooper, and he was mad. He asked me: "Boy, you got any guns in there?" I told him no. So, he offered me one of his. "**Here, take this un**!"

I went to Arkansas. I wanted to see what kind of people would elect Bill Clinton Governor. I couldn't vote for Clinton. I won't vote for anyone who can't operate **a joint correctly!**

Clinton said he didn't inhale. That would be like Monica **saying she didn't swallow!**

Did you see Monica Lewinsky had her own reality TV show? Turns out, **it blows too!**

Got booked in Canada again. Second time this year. I was happy. One show in Toronto for $1500, Canadian! Got back to America, it was worth **$42. Bleeping 50! Hey!**

(I had the second of a five joke bit poised, but the crowd lost focus. See what I did to rebuild focus. Again, if someone breaks the crowd focus by interrupting me, I swat them on the nose. It makes others in the crowd aware not to step on my material. You need to learn to make hecklers leave you alone. Deal with them firmly or they will kill some of your most precious jokes.)

Wow, thanks for interrupting me sir. I like your beard. Looks like you **went down on a goat!** Pardon me ma'am, I wasn't talking about you!

I live in Los Angeles, the Gay part of Los Angeles. Wearing red shoes, it's kind of hard sometimes. The other day, I'm trying to drive across town, I get caught in a Bisexual Parade! It was okay though, it broke up after like 15 minutes, because nobody knew **which way to go!**

Before I tell my next joke, I need one homosexual to walk out of the audience! Thank you sir!

(I usually avoid most profanity, unless it's needed. This is an active room. When someone exits the crowd and draws attention and focus, I make a big fuss of it, and continually refocus the crowd on me. Plus, I was prepared to refer to my active heckler as pussy-whipped, and I thought this joke would set that up.)

I got lucky, a comic friend of mine got sick and couldn't do his scheduled show in Las Vegas. So I got to fly in the morning, do one $500 show and fly out that evening. Boy, Las Vegas **has changed**! Really changed. Poor Siegfried and Roy! Poor Siegfried and Roy! Wow! Boy, you stay away from pussy, your whole life, and then one comes by and bites you on the head! What is that? Boy, Vegas **has changed!**

(Talk about the odd things that happen in your life.)

LA is crazy! In Los Angeles, they assign the freeway lanes according to your sexual preference! If you're single, then you're **in the Fast Lane!**

If you recently divorced, then you're in the next lane over…**with your blinker on!** (Feverishly signaling left with thumb gestures.)

The people weaving in and out of the lanes, they're the ones **cheating on their partners.**

If you're divorced, then you're way over in the slow lane, honking your horn needlessly.

There's a Gay Lane, but I hear: **It's a dirt road!**

(When you have a multi-joke bit, stack the jokes to reach a crescendo. The natural ending of the bit may cut out the need to segue, and then you can just dive into your next bit.)

I guess I'm old-school because I'm having trouble learning to use computers. Show me by round of applause if you use computers! As I'm struggling to learn, I have understood one thing: learn to use a computer or you **will not be able to buy any gasoline, food, sex, or DOPE!**

(At this point in my act, I use a subject that most in my crowd will relate to, and feel empathy towards me. Almost everybody is using a computer these days.)

So I got a computer, and a computer guru. He asked me what he wanted to do. I told him I wanted to surf the Internet. He said: "First, you have to log on." I told him: "I live in West LA, I wear red shoes, I'm straight, and **I don't log on nothin'!**

He said that's how you get connected, you gotta have a password. So, I learned about passwords. Hey did you hear about this? How does OJ Simpson log on the Internet? **Back slash, back slash, and back slash, escape!**

How does a gay man log on the Internet? **C, COLON, ENTER!** Hey, You've got male!

(Segues are for those amongst us who can't ride their current hunk's wave of laughs. Or you can preset a cue with the sound guy and let him fake surprise you. You look fearless!)

"Poor Lue's Almanac is a compendium of entertainment, information and words to the wise. Kinda like a Mad Magazine of social commentary! And now, from an undisclosed, secure location, it's time for Poor Lue's Almanac!"

(The only audio effect I use. The sound guy cues and plays the intro. It sets up my framework to do current topical jokes. This my performance piece, intended to show depth and draw applause.)

It's time for Poor Lue's Almanac! You got your red shoes on?? My motto is: The first part is true, the last part is Lue! My other motto is: hey, it's just a bird in the hand, **until you show it to some jerk!**

Here are the stories I'm working on tonight:

NASA goes to Mars, just to see if we can **keep Justin Bieber there!**

Archaeologists **uncover Cher's ORIGINAL breasts!**

And the LA Dodgers need a base-stealer, so they **trade for Winona Ryder!**

But the big story, still the big story is: "One Saddam down, one Osama to go! Now that things are going well, the administration changes the name from Operation Iraqi Freedom to Operation **WIN the damn election!**

The Iraqi owned, American operated, radio station in Baghdad has changed its call letters to W E 1. (As in, **WE WON!**)

The same Baghdad radio station has promised to not play any more Barbra Streisand music! Because… **haven't these people suffered enough?**

One note on the national front, it seems that California is now looking for **another migrant worker to govern the state!**

The American Guild of puppeteers has warned VP Dick Cheney to do a better job of **hiding the strings!**

I think you can tell I don't like our current president. I call him President Junior! I understand he graduated from two very fine colleges, so why is it that when he talks, he sounds like he graduated from **Yahoo A& M!**

As a matter of fact, George Bush Junior just had his second colonoscopy. All the doctors found was an **impression of his own head!**

And what is it with the Bush daughters? One got in trouble for pot, one got in trouble for pills. Who do these little tarts think they are? **Kennedys?**

One international note, India and its schizophrenic little brother, Pakistan, now have nuclear weapons! You know what this means, **7-Eleven controls the whole God damn world now!**

I'm not worried about India, its Pakistan that scares me! Their technology is so outdated their nuclear launch codes are **4G 5G 6G and 7G!**

In sports news, will Pete Rose ever get in the Hall of Fame?? **DON'T EVER BET on it!!**

Wheaties, breakfast cereal will honor the cryogenically preserved Baseball great Ted Williams, with their new **"EXTREMELY"** Frosted Flakes!

Unpredictable nutso boxer Mike Tyson's next outing will be sponsored by **PROZAC, ZANAX, and ZOLOFT!**

They're actually going to make ROCKY SIX! In Rocky VI, Sylvester Stallone fights **OSTEOPOROSIS!**

Closing sports with this: Two Buffalo Bill's football fans are on trial this week for being arrested while having sex during the football game last year! The defendant's excuse was: "We were the **only ones able to score for three quarters!**" Good Luck…fellas!

In biz news: Zena, Princess Warrior, has retired to become **CEO of Amazon.com.**

General electric has announced: if Pope Benedict dies, we will clone him! Because at GE, **we bring good things to life!**

The NRA, that's the National Rifle Association. The NRA has a new motto. Their new motto is: If it looks like a duck, and quacks like a duck**, shoot the son of a bitch!**

Procter and Gamble will merge with Tampax! **No strings** on the deal!

Celebrity sightings: have you heard about the new Lindsay Lohan Bail Bond Company? Hey, if we can get this crazy bitch outta jail, then **we can get anybody out of jail!**

Woody Allen is 78! So how many times does **78 go into 23?**

Rock 'n Roll super-star Mick Jagger is now 70 years old! That's **420 years old in Keith Richards's years!**

And tomorrow, on her TV show, Martha Stewart will show us all the **CORRECT way to make a Prison Bitch!**

Some sexual information: a new medical study shows that estrogen improves a woman's memory. Guys, that's why she can remember **EVERY stupid thing** you ever did!

Americans have more sexual partners than any other country! **We're number one! We're number one! We're number one! We're number one!**

There have been 69 deaths associated with the use of Viagra! And **DAMN NEAR a couple eyes put out!**

Closing the sex drawer with this: last week in Philadelphia, the police break up a prostitution ring working out of a Lens-Crafters store. Hookers at a Lens-Crafters store. Yeah, evidently you could have **been in and out, in and out, in and out, in and out, in about an hour!**

That's been Poor Lue's Almanac, signing off for this week…**Semper Funny, Y'all!**

(A five to nine joke hunk will set up your closing bit by increasing tempo.)

Okay, I've been here for about 20 minutes, and I'll admit it: I'm a weirdo! Can you tell? (Re-focusing) Yes ma'am, sitting at that table, I bet you know all about weirdoes.

I'm a weirdo because I don't get any sleep. I never get any sleep. I have to get up every night, late at night, to let my damn tomcat out. But, since I had his huevos cut off, he **goes out as a consultant now!**

I love my cat. I've had my cat for 10 years now. I'm tired of those string and yarn games. Now, I play mind games with my cat. Now, when I get my haircut, after the haircut, I've bend down, and I sweep all that hair on the floor into a bag. Then I take the bag of hair home… And dump **it right in my cat's bed!** "Take that, **you son of a bitch!** Your hair is **all over my stuff!**"

I don't think my kitty trusts me anymore since I've been putting those **Pop Rocks things in his litter box!** I'm getting a few blank looks on that one! Pop Rocks, it's a candy for kids, the kids put the candy in their mouths, and the moisture in their mouths makes the candy go snap and crackle! Then I give kitty **two** bowls of water. I grab my flash camera and wait by the litter box for the fun to begin! Little Kitty drinks the water, wets in the box: POW bang bang Meowww!

He didn't know whether to **hiss…or piss! Pee…or flee! Urinate…or evacuate!** *(My only rhyming triple couplet, vastly under-appreciated by non-poets.)*

(I involve the crowd with polls, then hit them with a faster pace, on a subject we can all relate to (sex) all the way to the finish. The effect I'm looking for is like sprinting to win a race! I'm trying to leave my crowd gasping for breath, and reluctant to see me go.)

Pardon me sir, I've gotta ask: Is this a date, or a marriage? Oh, a marriage, let's look closer. Ma'am, a personal question, are you still having sex? Look everybody, She went: "uh huh!" He went: "nuh uh!" **Maybe, you're not there, sir!**

You ma'am, a surprise sexual question: "When was last time you had a really major orgasm?" See everybody, she looked **right at her girlfriend!**

Can you feel the sexual tension in the crowd tonight?? **Except for you**, sir!

Let's get intimate, let's exchange some details: I have sex, do you have sex? Raise your hand if you have sex?! Wow, this must be a **dry county**! No, you sir, I'm not talking about farm animals! No, NO, no! **That's a baaaaaad joke**!

You ma'am, yes you raised your hand, but let's face it, it was **still vibrating!**

My Dad told me about sex. He told me that sex was just like your paycheck! **Enjoy it while you have it!**

I wrote my own book on sex, but of course it **was a handbook**! Like some of you folks, never even **thumbed through it!** Come on, guys, you tell me if **Palm** Sunday is not your favorite holiday!

I'm a golfer, and I think sex and golf are real close. My golf game is like masturbation! Satisfying to me, but **disgusting to those around me!** Hey, I bought a **new glove**! Anything to **shave a few strokes off**! Is anybody with me on this?

So I'm making love the other night, and after 20 or 30 minutes, Hey, I'm starting to get horny! **So, I hang up the telephone…**

Okay, let's take another sexual Poll. If you're in the crowd tonight and you are married, or if you've ever been married, show me by round of applause! Sounded pretty good. Boy that cost a few guys an elbow in the ribs!

I know the best part of being single. Do you know the worst part of being single?? Sleeping in that **wet spot…alone!**

Okay, if you're single, show me by round of applause. I think the **difference in enthusiasm…speaks for itself!**

Oh I forgot a group, I never want to forget this group, if you're in the crowd tonight and you been divorced, show me by round of applause. Wow, listen to that. Divorced people are pissed! Divorced people feel cheated! Divorced people **want some fun, right bleeping now, Mister!**

(As a middle act, I close with nine jokes in a row on the same premise. (Women!) The effect I'm looking for is empathy, agreement, and the crowd rooting for me to triumph in this crazy encounter. I just love this hunk of jokes. I don't close with it often, but this crowd laughed so much, I didn't have time, in a twenty-seven minute set, for my usual closer.)

I know how divorced people feel. I didn't want to get the divorce, I loved her. I didn't want to get the divorce, but **the guy she was sleeping with downright insisted!**

I married a strong woman. I love strong women. It's my belief that if it wasn't for the strong women in this world us stupid men would have burned the planet to a cinder long ago. If you're a man who has a strong woman in his life, you listen to her, you follow her advice, and you do what she says, or she will **break both your damn legs! Remember, you've got to sleep…sometime!**

I love strong woman. I married a strong woman. The woman I married was a Sgt. of Police from Tampa, Florida! I married a cop. What the hell was I thinking?

Let me tell you, it's hard being married to a female police officer. Is there any other man here that gets pistol whipped, **every time you leave that toilet seat up?**

It's hard sleeping with a police officer. Her gun, dammit, **it was bigger than mine!**

The last time we made love, she gave me a ticket **for going TOO FAST!**

I think what pissed her off, was that **rear end collision, though!**

She tried to book me for assault and battery, **with a DEAD weapon**!

It's OK! I told her, that the evidence… **Would not STAND UP in court!**

(Adios muchacho! A sincere, short goodbye and exit will often solicit more applause, because if the crowd is still laughing as they realize you're leaving, they may clap harder and longer.)

Thanks for having me, my name is Lue, thanks!

(I exited the stage straight to my headliner and warned him about the Bachelorette party and the bearded heckler. I told him the crowd would adore his act. Then, I went and thanked the owner/agent for my job. Mr. Sobel said: "It must be hell when they like you so damn much!" I smiled, turned and went to watch the headliner to analyze his chops. They both hired me again, twice the next year!)

If you can get more laughs out of a crowd, and you can explain how you did it, let me know. I'll be there to cheer you on! Your ability to do stand-up is a result of the choices that you've already made. Make better choices! By going modular you can find out what bits, jokes, or hunks have what effect in various places of your act. Always keep writing new jokes, so you will always have more parts to substitute in and out of your set. ***Edit yourself often, and choose your jokes wisely!***

Everybody these days thinks they're funny. I've seen a lot of unprofessional stand-up comedy. To be truthful, when I started, I did a lot of weak comedy myself. So, I watched the professionals, tried to write the same kind of jokes they did, and quite a few fellow comics tried to help me. Soon, some minor results proved I was getting funnier. If I can get funnier, so can you! I hope my tactics, techniques, and procedures make sense to you. Truly, as a stand-up, the only way to get better is to do it over and over. Do as many shows as you can, it gives you more chances to prove that you do know how to get funnier.

Once you've realized that almost all working stand-ups are funny, the next step for you is to prove that it might be preferable to work with **you**, instead of some other act. Stand-up comedy is the type of business that may require you to be charming every damn day.

The last lesson: I want to recognize and emphasize good manners and strong jokes. I want new comics to learn to analyze their acts logically, and be welcomed wherever they go. I want new stand-ups to be able to articulate themselves with clarity and passion. Those without good memories need not apply.

Against the backdrop of my career, I've tried to provide a context of what stand-up life was like to progress from a no-talent walk on, to a skilled speaker. (Who stayed continuously employed for 35 years.) I'm addicted to laughs! Standup comedy gave me a vocation and an endless chance to make new friends.

It's really going to be courage, drive, and your jokes that help you survive your first thirty shows. That means it's YOUR courage to believe you can be funny onstage, it's YOUR drive to find enough shows to get better, and IF your jokes make crowds laugh enough to forgive your slow learning curve. Everybody thirty shows old or less are amateurs. Give yourself, and all present at each of your shows, the definite advantage of being the most polite, most helpful amateur there that night! Many times, that's just who gets invited back. See, these methods are working…and that scores one for you!

I've learned to see life through funny colored glasses. After a lifetime of searching for laughs, and a career of sharing them, I'd do all it over again. Despite all the inherent rejections, endless peer put downs, and the lack of respect for touring acts, I'd do it again! It was that glorious for me. But, if I had followed the tips I've shared with you, I would have saved myself 5 to 7 years. I'd give almost anything right now, to have those 5 to 7 years back. I have learned that laughing gives back the things that life takes away. Never forget: Standup comedy is the result of the choices you make. Choose wisely!

It's a lot harder to stop doing stand-up, than to start doing it. I'm working now on the next book in my series: "How to be as funny as **you can be**!" It's for stand-ups that have gotten sixty to ninety shows experience. So, here's my offer: If you make it past your first thirty shows, and you need more help, find me. E-mail me. Snail mail me. Call me. I'll help if I can. Bust a lip! (Older comics don't say "Break a leg!" any more)

Good Luck, and may God Bless!

Curriculum Vitae

University of Texas: 1973-74 Radio, TV, film major, Co-founder Austin City TV

The Comedy Store: 1974 to 1983 Alumnus (MC, doorman, Video director, Improv director, Mitzi's boy)

Out of the Bag! 1975 to 1979 Heck & Deck Public Access Comedy show-30 episodes

L.A. Olympic Hdqtrs Staff-1984

Dept. Of Defense USO Tours: Pacific Command & Asia Command

Ollie Joe Prater: 1983 to 1990 (Opening act, tour manager)

National Touring act: 1983 to 2009 (Performed in 1000 cities in 10 years)

America's Funniest People: (ABC) 1995-three episodes

Cruise Lines: Carnival, Dolphin, Cunard, Royal Caribbean, Princess- 100+ voyages

The Cheers.org: 2007 to 2014 (weekly columnist, 83 articles, 15 million views)

Net Radio Live: Poor Lue's Almanac: 2008 Peabody Award nomination (62 issues)

CSPAN essay winner: 2008 "Please mute your TV!"

Comedyfox.com: 2008 to 2014 (original contributor)

Captions:

1) I finally found something that made me unique! I was booked over 40 times because of those red shoes. They didn't know my name, they didn't know where I was from. Bookers just asked around the road warrior circuits for the tall guy with red shoes, and then they found me easy enough.

2) Heck & Deck, young, undaunted, and dangerous, 1978 Hollywood

3) Heck & Deck, older, semi-daunted, and still dangerous! 2008 Hollywood

4). I traded a week of MC gigs to get this first headshot, and I never managed to look like this again. So, I used it for 10 years! I am the Stand-up Whisperer.

5) Because of my aging promo pic, my agent (Sobel) had two of his other comics kidnap me, and violently forced me to get a new headshot. I used this one for 10 years too!

6) OJ, in Tom Sobel's office, three months before he died. Carpe Diem, big fella!

7) Comedy Store Bombers-1979: On left, standing tall: Dave "Shoot it!" Letterman, Tim Reid, Lue Deck, Roger Van Pelt, Darrow Igus, Jimmy Walker, Johnny Witherspoon, and Tommy Dreesen. Kneeling, on left: Jimmy Heck, Joe Restivo, Darryl Mooney, Little person: Corky Hubbard, Dwayne Mooney, Littler person: Roger Behr, Jimmy O'Brien, and Bobby Kelton.

8) The TV director gave me this bumper sticker after my taping. I had suspected that I was amongst the funniest in our country, but now, I finally achieved documentation!

- See Lue's winning techniques in his video: "**100 Laughs**!" on YouTube! Search for Stand-up DECODED!

- Click on Lue's online column and articles at Thecheers.org and Comedyfox.com

- Check online for "Poor Lue's Almanac" A Peabody Award nominee for web joke-casts!

Semper Funny, Y'all!

LUE DECK
THE COMIC
IN RED SHOES

www.ingramcontent.com/pod-product-compliance
Lightning Source LLC
LaVergne TN
LVHW072050060526
838200LV00061B/4704